AWAKEN THE SLEEPER

THERE IS ONLY ONE TRUTH

Nick Castellano

Uhios Publishing, LLC
Mesa, Arizona

Published by Uhios Publishing, LLC
Mesa, Arizona
www.nickcastellano.com

All Bible quotes are from the King James Version unless otherwise indicated.

ISBN 978-0-9828475-0-3

Library of Congress Control Number: 2010932214

Printed in the United States of America
10 9 8 7 6 5 4 3 2 1

Cover design by Andrew W. Houglum (FonderConsulting.com)
Interior design by Mary Jo Zazueta (tothepointsolutions.com)

AWAKEN THE SLEEPER

This book is dedicated to everyone who has the "guts" to pursue their God-given purpose on this planet. It is dedicated to everyone who chooses to live as the Word has guided. And it is dedicated to those who choose to live as "victors" by taking responsibility for the circumstances in their lives.

This book is also dedicated to my wife, Michele, who helped guide me and walk by my side through this amazing growth period.

CONTENTS

CONTENTS

PREFACE

For forty years, things just "happened" to me. A situation would occur; I would react to it and then choose a proper course based on what happened. Sometimes good things happened; sometimes bad things happened. I simply lived with the results.

One spring day in Mesa, Arizona, I decided to create my day. I would happen to my environment rather than letting the environment happen to me. I was inspired by my pastor's teachings and books on quantum physics that I was reading.

That morning, I made a list of everything I was grateful for and I focused on the gifts I had been given to steward over: family, pastors, friends, house, car, etc. I felt grateful and thanked God for all He had entrusted to me. (Philippians 4:4) I was in joy, peace, and love—surrounded by *this environment I had created.*

Now that I had established the right environment (gratitude), I began to create my day. I told the day what it would yield for me and I saw it done in my mind's eye. I also felt the feelings "as if it were done." I saw myself as a millionaire.

Later that day, a stock I had received three years earlier for a product I helped create went public. The stock opened at $5 per share and went to $7 by the end of day. I owned 500,000 shares of this stock. I was a millionaire several times over in one day.

I was so amazed! I was in such joy! What I had been striving for all of my life was now mine—in one day—by creating it to be.

Did I do this? Was it luck? Was it a chance event finally paying off after years of hard work?

The next morning I woke up at four a.m. I was excited about what the day would bring—I mean, what *I* would bring to the day. I once again created an environment of joy, peace, and love by being grateful for all I was stewarding over. I saw myself in great wealth and peace.

I talked with God and said, "If I am correct in what I am doing by creating my day, please confirm this by some event that I had no part in producing. Please, let me know this is real. If it is real, I will teach others."

That afternoon, as I was driving in my car, a friend who is a wealthy doctor called my cell phone. He said I had been on his heart for three weeks. He had been given a directive by God to do something, but he was struggling with it.

I was curious, so I asked him, "What is your directive?"

My friend said he was directed by God to give me the two-acre plot of land across the street from my house. (I live in an upscale neighborhood at the top of a mountain in Arizona.) This lot had an appraised value of $1.2 million at the time.

I was crying so hard in joy, I had to pull over and stop the car. I was overwhelmed. I was creating my day and it was producing amazing results.

Why was this happening? Skepticism crept in. I am a trained Navy nuclear chemist and needed to find out why this was working before I could fully embrace the process.

This book is about my adventure to find God's truth in nature and how to apply His truth in all aspects of my life. It is written as a beacon of light to "shine the way" for all Christian warriors who are pursuing their God-given purpose in the Kingdom of God.

Through my personal story, Greek and Hebrew translations of the Word, and quantum physics, I will help you to realize that what you are going through, even if it is difficult, is exactly what must happen to help you find your path through your Godly purpose and step into your Kingdom Destiny.

When you feel crushed under the weight of your assignment and want to give up, you can feel rejuvenated with one of the greatest gifts one human can give to another: the gift of knowing that *you are not alone*. You are not now, nor have you been, the only person to go through pain and trials, to feel loneliness, to cry out to God for help and to hear nothing in response.

It is time to pick up your cross and pursue your purpose. In your purpose you will find all the fruits promised in the Word and that, in true relationship with God, your created environment on His planet can be one of peace, joy, and love.

"Awaken O Sleeper" the world needs your light as its intellect has brought it to the brink of destruction. Your "light and life" will guide the world back to that "common-union" with our Lord God through Jesus Christ.

This is a book of hope and a guide you can follow to reach your God-given purpose to find your Awakening.

The first step is to learn how to create an environment of joy, peace, and love.

INTRODUCTION

Awake thou that sleepest, and arise from the dead and Christ shall shine upon you and give you light.
(Ephesians 5:14)

Thy dead men shall live, together with thy dead body, they shall arise. Awake (O sleeper) and sing (shout), ye that dwell in the dust; for the dew (covering) is like the dew of herbs (prosperity), and the Earth shall cast out the dead. (Isaiah 26:15)

The church tells the newly saved, "Now that you are saved and in Christ you have all 'power, dominion, and authority'." By the Holy Spirit the newly saved must create and bring the Kingdom to their lives, their families, their church, and their world—but no one teaches them "how to" step into and wield this power they now possess.

Once we accept Christ as our Lord and Savior and we enter the Kingdom of God, all the rules change. What worked in the world no longer works in the Kingdom. We are now "joint heirs" in Christ Jesus and a new creation on this planet. (2 Corinthians 5:17) We were walking this planet as Homo sapiens subject to its rules and laws. But, now that we are in Christ, we are "Homo Kingdom"... a new creature, a new species, a subject of His Kingdom authority and Kingdom dominion; not the world's ways.

INTRODUCTION

Why, then, do we not step into this new power? Initially, it is because we still think we are the old person, not the saved person, so we act as children not knowing how to use our power. In Galatians 4:1 Paul said, "Now I say that the heir, as long as he is a child, differeth nothing from the servant though he be Lord of all." Galatians 4:3 says, "Even so we, when we were children, we were in bondage under the elements of the world." And in 1 Corinthians 3:1 Paul says, "And I, brethren, could not speak unto you as unto spiritual but as unto carnal, even as babes in Christ." (The word *carnal* is from the Greek word *sarkeeoos* which means "temporal unregenerated flesh.")

When we allow ourselves to be carnally minded, we are "babes" in the Body of Christ and cannot step into our inheritance. We are now spirit beings and we must act in the spirit by spiritual laws and our spiritual senses—not the five temporal senses.

Are you ready to begin your journey into spiritual maturity? I will use science, the Word, and all the truths I discovered to guide you on your way so that you too can utilize the power God has made available so that He may be glorified, bringing the Kingdom of God everywhere you step.

We will explore science and spirituality to see how both disciplines lead to only one conclusion: **There is only one truth!**

> *Our deepest fear is not that we are inadequate. Our deepest fear is that we are powerful beyond measure. It is our light not our darkness that frightens us the most. We ask ourselves, "Who am I to be brilliant, gorgeous, talented, and fabulous?" Actually, "Who are we not to be?" You are a child of God. Your playing small does not serve the world. There is nothing enlightened about shrinking so that other people won't feel insecure around you. We are all meant to shine as children do. We are born to manifest the glory of God that is within us. It's not just in some of us, it's in everyone. And as we let our own light shine, we unconsciously give other people permission to do the same. As we are liberated from our own fear, our presence "automatically" liberates others.*

Marianne Williamson (excerpt from *A Return to Love*)

AWAKEN THE SLEEPER

1.

DISCOVERY

There is only ONE TRUTH!

One of the great lessons I learned from studying the Word and quantum physics is "I had a choice." I could either let my day create the circumstances in my life, thereby turning over any power I may have had to the world, or I could step into my God-given creative abilities and create my day.

The biggest apprehension I had to creating my day was that I would have to take responsibility for the day I created. I could no longer assume the role of a victim. I could no longer believe that events and circumstances in my life were created by outside forces.

By assuming the role of creator, I would take responsibility for events and circumstance. And, once I took responsibility for them I stepped into "power" and with that power I could start to change my life "on purpose."

The challenge was: how do I consciously create the conditions I would like to have in my life and make it a reproducible process? (This thinking was from my nuclear-power training.)

In the spring of 2007, I decided to create a life that better lined up with what God wanted from me: the shalom life of being at peace, being whole, complete, and lacking nothing. This must be attainable or the Word would not speak of it.

I went out to the front porch, where I have a beautiful view of the city, and I got quiet in my body and spirit. I began to relax, breathing in through my nose and out through my mouth, until I was at peace and my mind slowed down.

I thought of God. Not a far away God, but my "papa." I am His son through Jesus and He loves me unconditionally. The Creator of the universe loves me? I am His son? These doubts ran through my mind for so many years. I now pictured myself outside the golden gates of heaven. I slowly pushed the gates open and as I walked forward a figure came walking toward me. It was a well-built man with dark skin and green eyes. His eyes fixed on me.

The Creator of the universe silenced all of heaven for me.

As I gazed deep into His emerald eyes, I saw a peace in them that was so complete I felt warm all over, as if that peace had embraced me. And in that peace, a love—a total love—for me! That man was Jesus. I embraced Him and hugged Him and He did the same to me. He said He had been waiting for me to come see Him. He was so excited that I had begun to realize who I was on the earth. He pulled out a white robe from under His robe and wrapped me in it. I thanked Him and kissed His cheek. He told me to go, that our Father was waiting for me.

As I continued walking, I began to gain confidence of who I was and that I was actually going to see God—my Papa! I entered the throne room and saw much activity: angels singing, cherubim standing guard looking very powerful, and God. God, the big powerful being on His throne, was discussing something with an angel, when all of a sudden He was aware of my presence. He turned His head slowly and looked at me. He smiled a warm, loving smile that covered me completely in acceptance and love. He moved His attention back to the angel and the singers and held up his right index finger to his mouth and said, "Shh, my son is coming."

I looked around for Jesus, but He was not behind me. I then realized that He meant me, not Jesus! The creator of the universe was silencing all of heaven because I was there. He, Jehovah, called me His Son!?!? I broke down and started to weep, overwhelmed by this and by the realization that He saw me as His son, just as if He was looking at Jesus.

God motioned for me to come forward, so I began to walk toward Him, wiping the tears from my eyes as I got closer. All the angels and cherubim in heaven were watching me as I took each step and there was total silence except for the sound of my footsteps. I looked up at His face beaming with love and joy, and I said a bit hesitantly, "Papa, can I sit on your lap?"

He chuckled and picked me up and put me on his lap. He said, "What would you like to do now, son?" I said I would like to create my day and do it with Him. He said that would be marvelous and He hugged me. We began to discuss the day as I desired it and the day as God would want it for me.

I do this meditation daily. As I wrote in the Preface, the first time I did this I became a millionaire in one day and it was all for the glory of God. For as Matthew 6:33 states "but seek ye first the kingdom of God, and His righteousness and all these things shall be added unto you."

Now that I have explained how I enter the throne room to speak with God every morning, let's discuss how you can create a reproducible process and forge a functional tool.

2.

SCIENCE

*In the beginning there was TRUTH;
Science and Spirituality were ONE!*

In order to change where you are at, you must receive, consider, and implement new concepts.

The purpose of this chapter is to expose the false teachings about our world. I will delve into the science of molecules, the atom, and the scientific theories that we have assumed are factual because they were devised and agreed upon by intelligent men.

I appeal to the intellectual but I will not go into such depth as to leave anyone behind. Please be open-minded when receiving these truths and know that what you know now has put you where you are today.

Basic Concepts

In the beginning there was Truth; science and spiritualism were one. There was only one truth and this truth emanated from one source. Man wanted to understand the planet he lived on and the nature of his creator, so man began to break down creation into smaller components to find the building blocks of living things.

SCIENCE

We termed this study *science*, which comes from the Latin word *scienctia* meaning "knowledge or knowing." Science is an attempt to discover and increase human understanding of how the physical (the visible) world works using controlled methods, data collection, and observations to construct theoretical explanations. To know God's creations would help man better understand the creator.

Over time, the Romans and Greeks utilized the theory that everything seen was composed of earth, air, fire, and water. (The Wiccans of modern day created a fifth element of "self.") The Greek philosopher Empedocles (495-435 BC) is credited with this theory. He was a poet, statesman, and physician—at that time these three practices overlapped each other and it was a natural co-mingling of what we would consider diverse studies.

This concept further supported the theory of *humourism*, developed by Hippocrates (460-370 BC), which states that the human body was composed of four humors which are in balance in a healthy person and each humor was composed of some or all of the aforementioned elements. The humors were black bile, which was composed predominantly of earth; yellow bile composed of fire; phlegm composed of water; and blood composed of all four elements. For centuries this theory was held true by Greeks, Romans, Muslims, and Western Europeans.

Over time, as science began to reduce the mysteries of God in the creation of this world, the church began to attack science (knowledge) and scientists (knowledge seekers) and called their theories *hearsay*. Hearsay is simply a proposed change to some system of belief, especially religious in nature, that conflicts with the previously established belief system. In the mind of the church, the religious belief system was being attacked and therefore those who studied science were ex-communicated or put to death for their pursuit of truth.

By the fourteenth century, science and religion had achieved a total split called *duality*. Each group would attack the other's way of thinking because they believed the truth was either one or the other theory and could not be both. Science, to explain itself, developed scientific theories while religion relied on faith in God's word, or at least what the religious men of that time thought the Word meant.

With the scientific approach that developed, many of the theories we live by today are believed as "fact." We will explore science and spirituality, and see how both disciplines lead to only one conclusion: "there is only one truth!"

Definitions

Let's define some basics so we can speak with a common language and understand what the different terms mean:

Atom – basic unit of matter consisting of a proton, neutron, and electron.

Molecule – stable, electrically neutral group of at least two atoms in a definite arrangement held together by strong chemical bonds. It retains the chemical and physical properties of the substance it makes up.

Energy – the amount of work that can be performed by a force. All energy is subject to the laws of conservation of energy (can be neither created nor destroyed, only altered in form).

Matter – has both mass and volume (takes up space). Matter is what atoms and molecules make up. The four states of matter are: solid, liquid, gas, and plasma.

Mass – the degree of acceleration a body acquires when acted on by some outside force. Property that causes a body to generate a gravitational field.

Proton – positively charged (+1) subatomic particle typically found in the nucleus of an atom.

Neutron – an electrically neutral substance particle typically found in the nucleus of an atom.

Electron – a negative substance particle typically found orbiting the nucleus of an atom.

Particle – a body that has spatial extent and internal motion and structure.

Charge – a calculated "theoretical value" of an individual atom after the electron density has been portioned against the atoms.

Theory – a unifying principle that can explain a body of facts and the laws based on these facts.

Thus, we know that in conventional science all matter is composed of molecules; molecules are composed of atoms; atoms are composed of subatomic particles called protons, neutrons and electrons; and all matter is made up of particles which are solid bodies with mass and volume.

> *Scientific theories are in a constant state of revision.*

Theories

We also know that a theory is a way to explain what is going on by unifying the laws and facts with a common thread. Let's discuss some of these theories briefly.

Atomic Theory – all matter is composed of units called atoms with a positive nucleus surrounded by negative electrons; atoms combine to form molecules.

Newtonian Theory – every particle in the universe attracts every other particle in the universe with a force that depends on the producer of the two particle masses divided by the square of the distance between them.

Bohr Atomic Model Theory – Bohr predicted electrons would occupy specific energy levels and each level could hold a finite number of electrons [$(F=GMm/d2)$].

Dalton's Theory - each element is composed of tiny particles called atoms and a pure element is composed of identical atoms; atoms determine the composition of matter.

Mathematical Theory – is the study of quantity, structure, space, and change developed through the use of *abstraction* and logical reasoning from counting, calculations, measurements, study of shapes, and motion of physical objects.

What We Know to Be True Today

How do these theories hold up today, with the improved sensitivity and technological advances of many of the measuring and monitoring devices that were not available to scientists in the past?

Problem #1: Detailed investigation by Nobel Prize winner Richard Feynman states that electrons can likely be found but this place cannot be pinpointed. In the electron cloud we discuss the "probability density" of an electron or wave function. Simply: an electron can act as a wave or a solid and cannot be pinpointed—only guessed at where it will be and in what form it will appear. This contradicts the **Bohr Atomic Model Theory** that depicted an electron much like the satellite of a planet orbiting it and allowing it to be found in a finite position.

Problem #2: Helium is a noble gas and composed of two protons, both with a positive charge; however they are not repelling one another. In fact, they are bound with two neutrons and two orbiting electrons. The binding of this positively charged nucleus had to be explained somehow so the term *nuclear forces* was created, which basically states that the force between nucleuses is much stronger than electromagnetic forces but drops off rapidly at distances greater than 10-13 cm.

Problem #3: In 1964, Murray Gell-Mann and George Zweig proposed that protons and neutrons were composed of energy packets called *quarks* (pronounced kwarks). Protons and neutrons, the particles that make up all matter, were now broken down into quarks or theoretical energy packets or particles. Two up quarks and a down quark is a proton. Two down quarks and an up quark is a neutron. A quark has never been observed, only theorized, so at this point the building block for all matter may be energy packets.

Problem #4: Gluons are hypothetical force particles, or energy, that bind quarks. This binding energy has nothing to do with any of the theories we have already discussed. Gluons possibly carry an electronic charge—but they have not been seen, only theorized.

Problem #5: Beta decay, which occurs when a neutron becomes a proton and an electron, which actually occurs when a down quark changes to an up quark, which also gives off anti-matter in the form of anti-neutrinos. (Even as a Nuclear Chemist I can not explain why this happens nor can anyone . . . it is just a theory.)

—————
Matter is just focused energy.
—————

Conclusion

Theories are in a constant state of revision, discoveries change what we thought we knew all the time. In fact, science even lost a planet in 2008 and downsized Pluto to a planetoid. How could that *fact* change?

With only a small amount of inspection utilizing modern equipment, we see that these basic concepts do not hold true on the subatomic level. What does this mean? Possibly that all matter is simply **focused energy bound together by thoughts and pre-conceived expectations of the observer.** Far-fetched? Out there? Am I saying that in the world of physics the human (observer) can create something in the seen world from the unseen? Possibly.

Theories continue to change. Here are a few that have changed over the past several years:

- Matter and Energy are different forms of the same thing.
- Before 1960 there were believed as fact four forces that acted as objects: Gravity, Electro Magnetic, Strong Nuclear, and Weak Nuclear.

- In 1960, electro magnetic and weak nuclear forces were combined (facts changed)
- In 1986, strong nuclear forces were combined with electro magnetic and weak nuclear forces. (Facts changed again)
- In 2005, the TOE (Theory of Everything) was proposed that all forces were just varying forms of one universal force. There is only one source of power and all power emanates from this source. (Starting to sound a bit spiritual when we say it that way)

In summary a theory is one way for man to *try* to explain what God has created and how it works. Mathematics is used to prove most of these theories as *supposed fact* and mathematics is defined as abstract and theoretical yet reproducible. Essentially we utilize a process theory to prove another theory, which we accept as fact—and more importantly truth. The **moment** we do this we ***weaken our abilities to create as spiritual beings.***

Let's leave this discussion and learn the true nature of God and His universe and how He asked for us to wield His power for Him as His heirs and joint heirs with Jesus Christ. We will see this through the experiments discussed in the next chapter.

3.

TESTING THEORIES

We create . . .

Theory 1: We create our world based on what we expect.

SPIRITUAL PROOF

For verily I say unto you, That whosoever shall say unto this mountain, Be thou removed and be thou cast into the sea, and shall not doubt in his heart but shall believe that those things which he saith shall come to pass, he shall have whatsoever he saith. (Mark 11:23)

Therefore I say unto you, What thing so ever you desire when you pray, believe that you will receive them and you shall have them. (Mark 11:24)

Through faith we understand that the worlds were framed by the word of God, so that things which are seen were not made of things which do appear. (Hebrews 11:3)

And the Lord said, If ye had faith as a grain of mustard seed, ye might say unto this sycamore tree, Be thou plucked up by the root, and be thou planted in the sea; and it should obey you. (Luke 17:6)

11

SCIENTIFIC PROOF

Particle Slot Wave Experiment:

In 1820, an experiment was conducted by physicist Thomas Young and supported by Nobel Prize winner Richard Feynman in 1964 (and many times since then) to prove that electrons were solid pieces of matter and that matter is created by particles. Initially marbles were shot through one slit. A screen was set up behind the slit and a pattern was formed on the screen. The pattern looked like this:

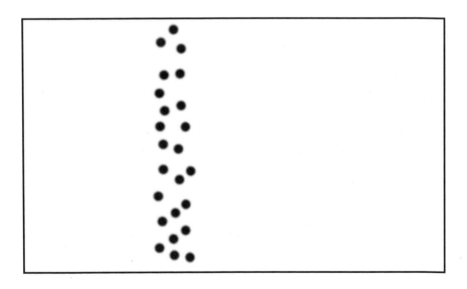

A second slit was added to the same steel sheet. The same screen was set up behind the slits. Below is the pattern formed on the screen by a solid piece of matter through two slits.

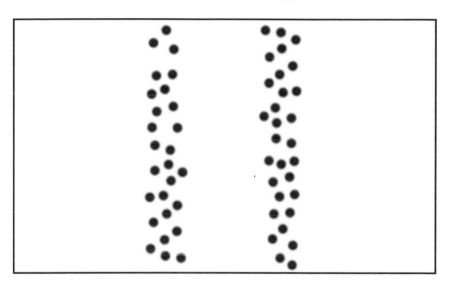

Initially that same steel sheet with one slit was placed in a pool of water. The wave-generated pattern was similar to the single slit with a solid line and looked like the diagram below:

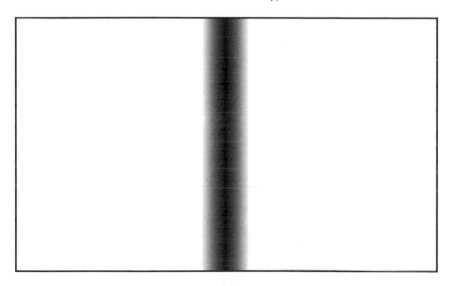

This same steel sheet was then placed in a pool of water with a second slit; waves were generated. The waves actually reacted with each other and formed an interference pattern on the screen that looked like this:

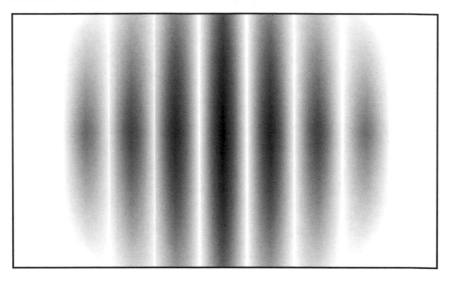

Now, let's go quantum.

The scientists created a slit screen on the atomic level and shot electrons through one slit. The pattern that formed on the screen was expected and very similar to the marble test.

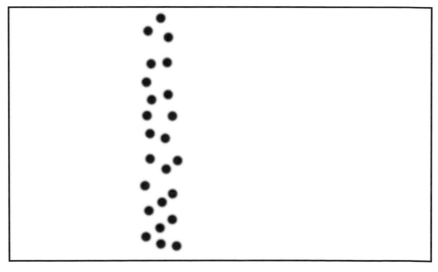

In the second experiment, scientists shot electrons through two slits—and something amazing happened. Instead of seeing the expected pattern:

Expected Pattern

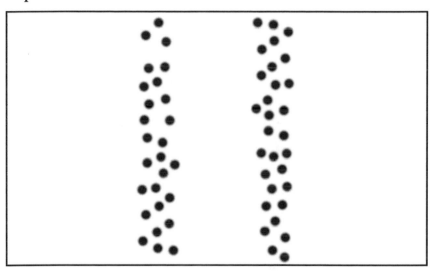

They saw the wave interference pattern on the screen. A wave pattern when solid electrons were shot? What happened?

Interference Pattern

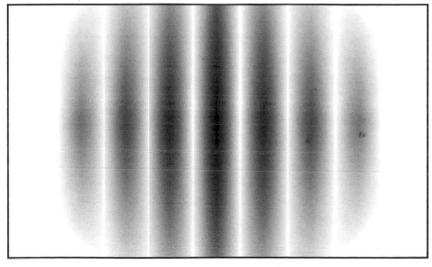

The scientists surmised that the solid electrons collided with themselves to cause this pattern. So, in the next experiment they projected the electrons one at a time to prevent particle interaction—and the same interference pattern occurred.

The scientists theorized that each electron reacted with itself, split into wave potentials, and thereby formed a pattern of thousands of "possibilities" on the screen. To ensure they were correct, the scientists decided to observe this phenomenon and installed a "measuring device" to see what was occurring.

The electrons were shot as before, one at a time; yet the result was now, amazingly, a "matter pattern"!??!

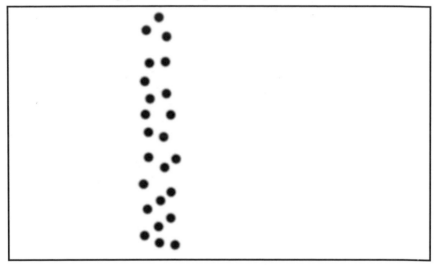

The scientists performed this test many, many times—with the same results. They then agreed that the electron (a supposed piece of matter) acted differently when observed than when not observed. Because it was observed and *expected* to be a certain way in a certain pattern (solid), it was. But, when unobserved it acted as a wave possibility.

Conclusion: Man's *observation and expectations* on the subatomic realm changed the outcome of the experiment, proving that man and his consciousness interacts differently, controls, and influences matter and its formation on the substance level.

Feynman went so far as to call the double-slit experiment a "Thought Experiment." Today scientists might conclude: Control your thoughts, control your world.

The Bible guides us to take our thoughts captive . . . "we begin to merge the two."

Theory 2: Time is not what it appears.

SPIRITUAL PROOF

While we look not at the things which are seen, but at the things which are not seen: for the things which are seen are temporal; but the things which are not seen are eternal. (2 Corinthians 4:18)

SCIENTIFIC PROOF

A student at Princeton University was placed in a booth and a recording was played. Beeps were copied onto a tape prior to the test at a 50/50 ratio. The tape was kept in a locked safe. According to the student's documentation, fifty percent of the sounds emanated to his left ear and 50% of the sounds emanated to his right ear. The student would raise his right hand if he heard the sound in his right ear and left hand if he heard it in his left. The results were recorded by the technician.

Later, the student was placed in the booth again to hear an identical recording. The same series of tests were run on the student except before the test started he was told there would be 25% more sound sent to his left ear than what his right ear would receive. The same tape was run, and as predicted, the student created 25% more left ear sounds than right ear sounds—even though the test was conducted at the same 50/50 split. Right ear and left ear sounds indicated the power of suggestion.

After the second test, scientists retrieved the original test tape from the vault and found, to their amazement, it was now producing 75% left ear sounds and 25% right ear sounds.

Conclusion: The student affected the tape and actually changed the locked up recording by his creative power; thus creating the theory of Time Reversal Symmetry: you can project your thoughts backward in time.

This tool has the power to change the labels you put on your past and the emotions attached to events. You can put a positive spin on your past so that when a similar opportunity arises in the future, you will not create the same negative emotions and negative cycle.

Theory 3: Words have power.

SPIRITUAL PROOF

For the word of God is quick, and powerful, and sharper than any two-edged sword, piercing even to the dividing asunder of soul and spirit, and of the joints and marrow, and is a discerner of the thoughts and intents of the heart. (Hebrew 4:12)

Death and life are in the power of the tongue: and they that love it shall eat the fruit thereof. (Proverbs 18:21)

SCIENTIFIC PROOF

Dr. Masaru Emoto performed a test at the molecular level by first photographing frozen water crystals in a plain bottle. There were no words or other information on the bottle. A baseline photograph was taken of the ice crystals; the crystals looked as expected.

Next. words of affirmation—"I love you," "thank you," and "you are great"—were pasted onto the bottle of water before freezing. Once the water was frozen photographs were taken of the crystalline structures. The crystals were beautiful and more magnificent than those in the baseline photograph.

Finally, the positive affirmations were removed and replaced with negative phrases like "I hate you" and "I want to kill you." Photographs were taken of the frozen water crystals. These crystals were ugly, deformed, and dwarfed in appearance.

Conclusion: This experiment proves words have power over water crystals and affect the beauty and functionality of the crystal. The human body is composed of approximately 72% water. What affect do our words have on others? What affect do our words have on our selves?

Finally, brethren, whatsoever things are true, whatsoever things are honest, whatsoever things are just, whatsoever things are pure, whatsoever things are lovely, whatsoever things are of good report; if there be any virtue, and if there be any praise, think on these things. (Philippians 4:8)

Words have power!

Theory 4: We have the power to heal ourselves.

SPIRITUAL PROOF

What? Know ye not that your body is the temple of the Holy Ghost which is in you, which ye have of God, and ye are not your own? (1 Corinthians 6:19)

Who his own self bare our sins in his own body on the tree that we, being dead to sins, should live unto righteousness: by whose stripes ye were healed. (1 Peter 2:24)

Likewise reckon ye also yourselves to be dead indeed unto sin, but alive unto God through Jesus Christ our Lord. (Romans 6:11)

He sent his word, and healed them, and delivered them from their destructions. (Psalms 107:20)

For the truth's sake, which dwelleth in us, and shall be with us forever. (2 John 1:2)

SCIENTIFIC PROOF

A study was conducted on one hundred Parkinson's patients in a large hospital in India who had a lack of Dopamine in their system. They were told that they were being given a new state-of-the-art drug that cures Parkinson's disease by producing Dopamine. In reality, they were given placebos (sugar pills). In three weeks of testing, 50% of the patients showed no external signs of Parkinson's disease and subsequent blood tests revealed Dopamine was being produced in their bodies.

Conclusion: The human body has the ability to heal itself based on what we believe to be true. Likewise, the human body can make itself sick based on our beliefs.

The level of empowerment you want when it comes to healing and good health is your choice.

Theory 5: We are interconnected (entangled) with other humans. We are not separated by our physical bodies or distance.

SPIRITUAL PROOF

And the LORD said, Behold, the people are one, and they have all one language; and this they begin to do: and now nothing will be restrained from them, which they have imagined to do. (Genesis 11:6)

I have even from the beginning declared it to thee; before it came to pass I showed it thee: lest thou shouldest say, Mine idol hath done them, and my graven image, and my molten image, hath commanded them. (Isaiah 48:5)

The Lord possessed me in the beginning of his way, before his works of old. (Proverbs 8:22)

They are created now, and not from the beginning; even before the day when thou heardest them not; lest thou shouldest say, Behold, I knew them. (Isaiah 48:7)

SCIENTIFIC PROOF

A random-energy generator measures amounts of energy in a certain area. In 1995, during the OJ Simpson trial in Los Angeles, random-energy generators were set up in three different locations around the United States. Prior to the verdict, energy levels began to rise. When the verdict was announced on October 3, 1995, random energy increased threefold on each of the energy-measuring devices from the normal baseline levels.

The funeral of Diana, Princess of Wales, on September 6, 1997, was viewed worldwide by an estimated 2.5 billion people. A large spike in random energy was observed by random-energy generators at the time the funeral was held.

By September 2001, eighty-seven random-energy generators were placed throughout the world; all the devices were operating. On September 11, 2001, three hours prior to the first airliner crashing into the Twin Towers, the random-energy generators throughout the world began to spike. Just prior to the first airliner attack, the random energy throughout the world was six times higher than normal.

Conclusion: We are all entangled and connected—separateness is an illusion caused by the limitations of the physical body. As a species, we have precognitions when something big is going to happen. Whether you like it or not, we are not alone! We all come from one source—God—and He is in everything and through Him we are connected.

Theory 6: We have the power.

SPIRITUAL PROOF

Verily, verily, I say unto you, He that believeth in me, the works that I do shall he do also; and greater works than these shall he do; because I go unto my Father. (John 14:12)

SCIENTIFIC PROOF

In July 1994, a group of Christians in Washington DC went to the Chief of Police and said they would like to help bring crime down 20% that evening. The Chief said the only way that would happen in July, in Washington, was if a blizzard occurred. A group of one thousand Christians gathered in a local park and focused and prayed on the reduction of crime. All night they prayed and were of one accord in the belief that they could decrease the crime rate.

To the amazement of the Chief of Police, the crime rate dropped 21% in that 24-hour period—and not one snowflake fell.

Conclusion: When we focus on our creative power and "the waves of possibilities" we can and do create our future. You are a creative being created in God's likeness and image and made of the soil of the earth. You are put on this earth as a spirit being in a body to have all power, dominion, and authority over it. We are the earth's stewards and its kings and priests. Just by our words, expectancy (hope), and actions (faith) we create the reality we live in. Not always good but always fair based on our true beliefs.

Some of you will not believe these experiments or the science behind them because if you did, then you are responsible for your life. With great power comes great responsibility.

Some would rather believe what the government, the media, and religion tells them: that they are victims and have no responsibility in their fate or the direction of the world or that "God will save them one day from this terrible earth." God has already saved us through Jesus and he expects us as stewards of his Kingdom and his children to wield the power he laid up for us to act like "the salt" and "the light" to this and for this world. Things do not happen to you … you happen to things!

You see, playing the victim has its perks. You make no decisions and are never wrong. Others will have to care for you. When assuming this victim role, are you shining out your abundant God? Will He say to you, "Well done my good and faithful servant!"?

Don't check out and be a victim—become a victor.

"The harvest is plentiful but the laborers are few."

Most people don't positively affect their reality because they don't believe they can. You can, you must, you do!

"AWAKE O SLEEPER." You are in charge of what you have now and what you will create for the Kingdom in the future.

4.

CREATING BY FAITH

Everything is composed of energy and energy pulses in waves.

All matter is made up of energy; there is truly "no matter," which is "what's the matter" with the theories based on matter.

Everything is composed of energy and energy pulses as waves. You, me, a tree, a dog, a car, etc., are composed of energy-emitting waves. Waves have amplitudes and frequencies and attract to one another. Nikola Tesla understood this law and determined that each thing has a harmonic frequency that it exists at. For example, the earth has a harmonic frequency of 7.8 hertz.

Every thought you have is composed of thought waves or vibrations. Your entire body vibrates with these thoughts which travel along with speed, force, and intensity based on your belief in that thought. These waves align with like waves and attract like things to edify this thought pattern.

A thought firmly fixed in your mind will attract the things represented by that thought. Thus, if you think negative thoughts, you will attract negative events, people, and circumstances and reinforce your negative thoughts. If you focus on peace, love, and joy, you will attract people, things, and situations that reinforce your state of peace, love, and joy.

Words are more powerful than thoughts. The word is a focused thought. A word is like light focused into a laser. It has power to create. Words have great energy and energy affects matter since all matter is energy. What you speak in faith over and over, you create. Are your words about good positive things or fearful negative things?

You create your reality.

In the quantum arena, in every person's life there is an infinite number of possible results that could occur. These possibilities are called *quons*. Quons are waves of potentials or *possibility waves*.

In a normal energy wave (light), the amplitude (height) of the wave square is considered the "energy of the wave." A quantum wave (quon) has an amplitude and frequency but no energy (your focus on the event gives it energy). In the case of a quon, its amplitude square is equal to the probability that it will be created or made visible or be pulled from the unseen into the seen.

When quons are focused and a specific circumstance is talked about, the speaking gives energy to the quon until it starts to exist in the visible world as hadrons, quarks, and electrons. These sub-atomic particles can be measured as sources of energy and the only thing that has brought them into the physical world are the focused thoughts and words you put toward the circumstance or situation.

If you create your world in an environment of love, peace, and joy you will create things that bring love, peace, and joy (Kingdom Environment). If you do not focus on this creation process, you are in a **"fate"** environment, which is sometimes good and sometimes bad. You have no control; you have become part of someone else's creative process.

If you create from lack, fear, and stress, you will produce results that keep you in lack, fear, and stress. You create a negative environment by your focus on it. It is not about what is fair it is about the emotional environment you create from and what your expectations are.

You create your own reality based on the thoughts and intentions of your heart and the power of your words—every time, no exceptions!

Let's take this concept and see if any of what science believes is written in the Bible.

First we must understand that God created all things visible (seen) and invisible (unseen) by His word. Colossians 1:16 states: "For by him were all things created, that are in heaven, and that are in earth, visible and invisible, whether they be thrones, or dominions, or principalities, or powers: all things were created by him, and for him."

What does science say about this? Scientists calculate that 23% of the universe is dark matter and 73% is dark energy. Thus, 4% of what has been created as matter can be seen in light. Only 4% is visible to the human eye!

This creative process assumes that what you are focusing on and giving your power and energy to you must want.

So, we "intellectuals" make decisions, small and large, based on 4% of what exists in the universe, i.e., that which we can see. And, we know for a *fact* that we are correct in making these decisions. Is this maybe why we make so many bad decisions?

The most foolish people in the universe, we call them intellects, and I am one, make decisions with their five senses and we follow blindly calling "what they have declared factual information for fear of being thought of or called a fool." Who is the fool? Use the tools God has given you to overcome those bleak times when the world needs your ability to see what cannot be seen and create what has not yet been created in the visible realm.

I would venture to say the true answer to our decision-making ability and power comes from the individuals who make their decisions based on the 96% unseen, "the gut" or guidance from the Holy Spirit. These are the wise and the wealthy using both seen and unseen as the source of their decision-making abilities.

Let's go back to the Word and do some Greek translation. In Hebrews 11:1 it states, "Now faith is the substance of things hoped for, the evidence of things not seen."

Christians know this Scripture and understand it to mean that by our faith things come into this world.

Let's translate this Scripture from the Greek:

English	Greek	Greek Translation
Now	de	now, (faith is now, God is "I am")
Faith	pistis	belief
Is	esti	makes up or consists
The substance	hypostasis	essence, nature of things, properties
Of things		that make up things
Hoped for	elpizo	expected
The evidence	elegohos	proof
Of things	pragma	matter
Not seen	blepo	looked on by the natural eyes

When translated from its original Greek, Hebrews 11:1 reads: *"Now (the only time faith works is in the "NOW") belief makes up the properties of a thing expected and is proved by the manifestation of matter not previously seen by the naked eye."*

Faith is the building block of all matter seen in this realm. Faith is the substance (energy) in the unseen that all things are made from. Did God know quantum physics? Maybe we are discovering how God works through quantum physics? Maybe??

So, what actually happens when we "act in faith" in the scientific realm? Quantum physicists explain that in this visible reality, when an energy wave's amplitude is squared, that indicates the energy of the wave. That is fine.

A quantum physicist would say there are millions of quantum waves or probability waves or quons available for each circumstance and situation you experience. A quon's amplitude squared will equate its probability of being brought "from the unseen world to this seen world." What you focus on and believe and the amount of positive or negative energy you put around that event will dictate what and how quickly it is pulled from the unseen (invisible) to the seen (visible). Quantum physics calls this "collapsing the quiff."

You have a choice on the energy you give to the event or the label you put on the event (good or bad) and what you are focusing on regarding the event. If you focus on a positive outcome in an environment of love, joy, and peace (the Kingdom environment) and your focus is performed in hope (assurance that it will be done), and this is followed by the action step of faith (acting and feeling as if it were already done), you will collapse the quiff and bring the unseen positive event into the seen.

Or you can choose to vibrate in indifference, a what-will-be-will-be place. Sometimes positive outcomes will occur; sometimes negative outcomes will occur, thereby reinforcing the *indifference* state of *qué será será*. Or you might choose—yes, it is a *choice*—to vibrate from an environment of fear, lack, and stress and focus on negative results by hoping (wishing) it does not happen. Just the focused energy in a "not" state will bring a negative result into this visible realm and edify and support your vibration state of fear, lack, and stress and help keep you there. Why? Because you create from that place in choice so the process of creating assumes you want to stay

> **. . . you were the common factor at every incident in your life.**

there. This creative process assumes that what you are focusing on and giving your power and energy to, you must want. It was set up for a creature of power, dominion and authority yet this incorrect focus results in creating more of the lack you are focusing on in your life.

This process works every time and if you can truly control the environment you create in and the focus of your energy then you can create a great life for yourself and your family all to God's glory. If you choose to focus on negative and lack things you will continue to bring these things into your reality and "what a dark light you will be to the world." (Matthew 6:23) And, if you choose to play the role of victim, i.e., stuff just happens to me, then sometimes positive will occur and sometimes negative and there will be little difference between your fruit and the fruit of the world.

You can't fake a place of peace, joy, and love and think you will receive anything. Your heart and your head must vibrate in unison, lined up with God through Jesus Christ, in peace, joy, and love. God told us to focus on these things and He told us a double-minded man is unstable in all his ways (Philippians 4:18) and we should expect nothing when we are creating (James 1:8) as a double-minded man. In Galatians 6:7 the Word says, "God will not be mocked; for whatever a man soweth, that shall he also reap."

In His Word God tells us to repent, which means to "think differently and do differently." If what you are doing now is working and showing out the glory of God in your life then change nothing. If you are constantly coming near to creating success but never seem to get there then repent and create greatness in your life for His Kingdom *on purpose*, not by chance. You have been given all power, dominion, and authority on this earth to shine out the glory of your God. Do not faint or find a place of comfort where you can blame (disempower) someone else or a system or a company.

You have created your life to this point; you were the common factor at every incident in your life. You were at every crime scene. The exciting thing is that you can now intentionally and on purpose create a bright future for you, your family, and this world that God so loves. When do you think would be a good time to implement and create this way in your life? As always, the time to start is NOW!

5.

INFLUENCING YOUR CREATIVITY

"If you don't know who you are you will naturally fit in and line up with other's vibrations."

The electro encephalograph (EEG) is a machine that monitors brainwave activity. There are four basic types of brainwaves: beta, alpha, theta, and delta. CDs and DVDs emit these waves for many different purposes. Brainwaves can be influenced externally to aid your body and soul to line up and vibrate with what you are creating. Try the following in your meditations:

Beta Waves (alertness, focus, and cognition): Beta waves exist at a frequency of 14 cycles per second and above. They exist in the conscious mind when your attention is focused on the outside world. They are associated with peak conversations, heightened alertness, and visual activity. This is a typical wave pattern of a person in normal day-to-day interactions.

Alpha Waves (relaxation, visualization, and creativity): Alpha waves exist at 8 to 13 cycles per second and are present during dreaming and light meditation with the eyes closed. In alpha, we begin to access the wealth of creativity that lies just below the conscious mind. It is the gateway into our deeper consciousness.

This is the range of waves that the earth's electromagnetic field resonates at, called Schuman Resonance.

Theta Waves (intuition, listening to the Holy Spirit, meditation, vision, imagery): Theta waves exist at 4 to 7 cycles per second and are typical in sleep or a high meditation state. This realm is for deep thought, when focus is on the inner self and improvement not on the outer world. Theta meditation increases creativity, enhances learning, reduces stress, and awakens intuition in one's self.

Delta Waves (deep sleep, healing, and detached awareness): Delta waves exist at frequencies from 0.5 to 3 cycles per second during deep sleep and deep meditation. These waves create a total vacation from our visible world and create great peace and tranquility inside the body. Delta waves are responsible for the release of growth hormones which heal the body.

Using the law of wave attraction, listen to sounds that produce the type of waves you require to line up with the consciousness level you want to achieve. The brain begins to vibrate at the same frequency of the rhythmic sounds you are listening to; thus you can produce desired results much more quickly when listening to specific waves. Everything moves at a beat in a rhythm, find the proper rhythm and find peace.

I use this tool whenever I want to write. I know I want to be in an alpha or theta state, so I tap into the spiritual realm by listening to CDs of alpha-theta sounds of nature or instrumental music that emit alpha-theta waves. I play the CD throughout the house. Typically in about five minutes I am very relaxed, in a creative state, and I begin to write. My body and mind line up with these waves and in no time I am vibrating at the same frequency as the music and easily enter into a creative state.

This same principle applies to the thoughts, the people, and the environment you surround yourself with. If your surroundings are vibrating with people who are in a state of lack or fear, and constantly complaining and you are not aware of your state, then you too will begin to vibrate with them and you will soon find yourself complaining and in fear and worry.

If you want to change the circumstances in your life then change who you spend time with. Change who you call your friends, who you vibrate with, or at the least remove them from your inner circle of influential friends. If you want wealth and confidence in your life then surround yourself with wealthy confident people. You will begin to vibrate at their frequency and attract what they attract. Truly, if you want to know who you are, look to see who you spend your time with.

> *If you want to change the circumstances in your life then change who you spend time with.*

When you spend time with God the Father, you vibrate at the frequency of peace and joy and walk in the power of love. When you believe and realize who you are and Whose you are, you vibrate with Him and walk in all power, dominion, and authority as Jesus did. Jesus would walk into rooms of sinners (Pharisees, Sadducees, prostitutes, tax collectors) and change the environment based on His vibration with Father God and knowing that He knew who He was. The entire room would shift and line up with Jesus' frequency. They could suddenly see and would repent of all sin and follow Jesus.

If you don't know who you are, you will naturally fit in and line up with others' vibrations. But, when you know who you are and believe it in your heart, the strength of your vibration will force others to line up with you or they will leave the area.

We are environment changers! When you spend time with God, you have all power, dominion, and authority. People, situations, and circumstances will line up with you because they know instinctively that you know WHO you are and who you represent.

6.

PHYSICAL VIBRATION

Your frequency or thinking attracts and aligns with like frequencies.

We have touched upon frequencies and vibrations and have said that everything that exists vibrates at a certain frequency, even the earth itself. We also know that we vibrate at a certain frequency.

Our body resonates at a frequency which varies based on our emotions and the focus of those emotions. Your frequency, or thinking, attracts and aligns with like frequencies (the Law of Attraction).

We also know that these frequencies can pass through what we would consider solid objects with no hindrance or alteration to them and can travel around the world. They do not dissipate unless we change our vibrational state and they attract like frequency things and align with them to reinforce the vibrational state of the sender (the Law of Attraction). Let's talk on this in more detail.

Your brain does not know the difference between what it sees or what it creates. Based on the vividness of the image you create, the emotion tied to that image, and the strength of your belief in that image, your brain can be manipulated to think a situation, circumstance, or thing already exists. When this meditative focus and belief exists in its creator—you—then you will attract situations, circumstances, and things that reinforce your belief state or your vibrational state.

On the physical realm, this is what causes the vibration of the body. An event is focused on and a "label or definition" you create for that event is applied to the event [good, bad, awesome, sad, amazing, terrible, grief, etc.]. Once your mind labels an event, the hypothalamus of the brain releases the appropriate neuropeptides (based on the emotion of the label). The neuropeptides "keylock" into every cell of your body at the cells' receptor sites for this emotion or this chemical released by this emotion.

What we believe in our heart we receive in our world.

Based on this chemical reaction, your body vibrates at a certain frequency at the cellular level. If the label you put on the event was fear, then your entire body vibrates at a lower frequency of fear and begins to attract things into your life that edify this state of fear. More thoughts and things that cause fear come into your mind and you can quickly descend into an abyss of fear based on this initial vibration or label you put on the event. One thought leads to another and another and soon fear circumstances appear in your life until fear is all you can see or attract. You are overwhelmed by the fear *you have created* in your life, based on your focus and belief in the label you put on the event.

An example of this could be when you get a big bill in the mail or some bad news about a loved one. "Bad luck comes in threes!" was one of the confessions in our house as I was growing up. So, we all just waited for two more bad things to occur. We were all vibrating at the lower frequency attracting what we considered "bad things" into our life—and you know what? We always got the other two. We would then resume our normal life of *qué será será*.

You can also choose (that's right, *choose*) to put a positive, joyful, peaceful, or loving label on the same event. You can believe that every time this circumstance occurs, a great blessing follows. At this point, you focus on the coming blessing. You are excited by the anticipation of the blessing you know will occur and you embrace it. You label the event with joy, thereby causing the hypothalamus to release different neuropeptides, and the chemical reaction of joy is created causing you to vibrate at a much higher frequency and aligning with and attracting more joyful thoughts and attracting situations, persons, and things which further edify joy and the belief you have in that joyful place you created.

Philippians 4:8 states: "Finally brethren, whatsoever things are true, whatsoever things are honest, whatsoever things are just, whatsoever things are pure, whatsoever things are lovely, whatsoever things are of good report, if there be any virtue and if there be any praise, think on these things." (The Greek word for "think on" is *logizoma* which means "take an inventory, esteem and focus."

The Bible also talks about our thoughts and how we should control them and take them captive. It seems God knew about how all things worked and the science behind all things and He was teaching us "how to" utilize this world He created by teaching us the how-to's of a great life in the Kingdom of God. This is not New Age or quantum physics. Those are simply labels man has put on processes God set up from the beginning of time and man uses these labels to define these processes to make them more about man and his greatness and less about God. This process is simply how God set up this planet for his children. What we believe in our hearts, we receive in our world.

The Word is not dead, it is alive and constantly teaches us how to walk this planet like His son did and how to walk in the reclaimed power, dominion, and authority Jesus has given us. Maybe knowing how the process works will help us more effectively use this tool God has given us and walk like Kings and Priests on this earth and become empowered—finally walking as "The Sons of God."

7.

ADDICTIONS

*You help no one, not even yourself,
if you choose to play the victim.*

We are all addicts! A bold but true statement. Every one of us is addicted to something. It may be a socially acceptable addiction, such as requiring praise or approval from others, or being part of a team or group. It doesn't matter if the cravings have a positive or negative label—they are addictions.

Each day we must meet our biochemical needs for the addictions we have acquired and developed. Drugs, alcohol, and smoking are physical addictions; as are victimization, sex, fear, distrust, control, arrogance, and even STRESS. That's right. People can be addicted to stress.

Basically, if you can't control your emotional or physical state, then you are addicted to it. This is not a condemning statement, it is an empowering statement. Your body creates a physical need for an emotional state so that the neuropeptides keylocking with the receptor sites of your body's cells can produce the desired chemical reaction. Over time, you become addicted to the chemical produced by that emotional state; so naturally you want, no *require*, to be in that state as quickly as possible—even if that state is not beneficial to you.

Alcoholism and drugs are chemical addictions that are developed as the result of an emotional addiction, i.e., an emptiness, a lack, or a "hole in the soul" that we are trying to fill. One may think if he can stop drinking he

All addictions ... can only be conquered when they are turned over and released to a higher power.

can remove the emptiness and defeat the addiction—but any alcoholic will tell you this is not the case. We just become "dry drunks," miserable in our daily lives because we have not controlled the source of our need to drink. All reformed alcoholics and drug addicts know that only when there is a complete surrender to a higher power (in my case, God) will the physical and emotional addictions be broken.

All addictions, both accepted and unaccepted by society, can only be conquered when they are turned over and released to a higher power. Relationship with Him is the key that breaks these addictions—no matter what it might be. As you spend more time with God, the bonds of physical, chemical, and emotional addictions break down and you are set free.

Now that you know this on a conscious level, or more simply put "it has been brought into the light," you can change it. Or you can pretend you don't know a thing, play the victim role, and continue to get the same things you have created all of your life. It is your choice. Do you want to be a victim or a victor? You help no one, not even yourself, if you choose to play the victim.

A victor creates his day and infinite possibilities for his tomorrows by focusing on positive expectations and controlling his emotions. Are you willing to change? Are you willing to become the powerful being you were created to be?

Choose life!

8.

IT IS NOT ABOUT YOU

*The key to becoming entangled with
others is simply the intention to do so.*

Entanglement is the theory that at some level we
are all connected, that we all come from one source and are part
of one another. Albert Einstein could not agree with this theory
because he said, "if entanglement and Quantum mechanics be
true then this would require 'spooky action' at a distance." What
Einstein meant by this is that he couldn't believe that any psychic,
mystic, or Holy Spirit experience could happen. It didn't make
"common sense" (didn't compute using our five natural senses).

The key to becoming entangled with others is simply the intention to do so. Experiments conducted at the University of New
Mexico entangled friends whose intent was to become more
entangled with each other. The study involved measuring their
brain activity with an EEG machine. In one room, an individual saw light flashes. His brain activity was measured. In another
room, the "entangled partner" experienced the same brain activity in his EEG measurements even though light flashes were not
occurring in his room. (This experiment has been recreated many
times in London by Peter Fenwick.)

The point is that no matter how real our physical separation may be, separation is an illusion. When we allow ourselves to get intimate with other people, we can feel their feelings and sometimes read their thoughts. We can communicate with them on so many levels that we allow ourselves to "become one."

For example, when a truth is revealed or a new truth discovered, you might think you are the only one who received or faced that truth; however, days or weeks later, from across the country, you see someone else discuss the same topic, the same revelation, the same truth that you thought you had found. The truth is everyone received it! A very few chose to embrace it and fewer decided to do something about it, but the human race received it.

Oftentimes the Holy Spirit reveals a concept, idea, or truth and the Christian does little or nothing with what he received. Later, the Christian learns that someone else used the idea— and succeeded with it. The world knew the idea was good and did something about it; unlike the Christian who questioned, "Is this from God? How can I do it? I need money!" Etc., etc. The point is that the information from the Holy Spirit was soon known by all due to our connection as the human race, our entanglement.

> *Regardless of belief, mankind is entangled.*

Humans resonate at a certain frequency or level of consciousness "As One." When we help our fellowman the resonance increases to a higher level toward joy and love. When we take advantage of or hurt another we hurt all mankind, including ourselves. The Lord gave us the greatest command: "Love God with all your heart, mind, soul and strength and love your neighbor as yourself." When you love your neighbor as you love your God, you are essentially loving yourself. All mankind vibrates at a higher frequency. We become closer to God.

We, as the Body of Christ, are connected through the Holy Spirit and can do great works if we move As One. As the human race we are also connected through the "Spirit of Man" thus we cannot justify not loving all men unconditionally because they

Separation is an illusion.

were created by God, as unique and individual as fingerprints. My God wishes "that none should perish and fall short of the glory of God."

When you help someone and love someone, you help and love yourself. When you hurt someone, lie about them, slander them, talk about them in a derogatory manner you are also hurting yourself.

Do you see yourself as part of a whole and as the Body of Christ as part of all Human beings or as an individual involved in only self? Regardless of your belief, mankind is entangled.

9.

THE FIVE R'S

Recognize that God exists.

Now that I have discussed science, spirituality, quantum physics, waves, and attraction, I will teach you the Five R's on how to apply this knowledge to bring the unseen to the seen.

Relax physically and emotionally to create an environment of joy, peace, and love. In this relaxed state you are vibrating at the highest frequency and creating positive energy. In this environment you will attract things into your life that bring joy, peace, and love to you. Don't stop reading. This is not New Age, it is the Word and how it works. How do you get to this relaxed state? Slowly breathe in through your nose and out through your mouth for ten to fifteen minutes or however long it takes for you to become "quiet." You cannot pretend to be relaxed. If you have inner tension, it will nullify your creative power (James 1:6-8).

Recognize that God exists and He has all power, and through Jesus Christ He has given us stewardship of this planet, and this stewardship is best served when we work jointly with God and each other. You must recognize that we are surrounded by God and God is in everything. God is in each of us and He created everything through the Word. All things are held together by His mighty Word. You must recognize that we were given all power, dominion, and authority on this planet through Jesus Christ and we were created in God's likeness and image. Therefore you have creative power in you and working through you.

You must recognize that we have the answers to all of life's questions through the Holy Spirit. This is a hard concept to grasp because most people like to go to the victim statement "I don't know." Therefore, you must seek the Holy Spirit's guidance and listen to that small voice within you. You must recognize that we never create anything from nothing. God allows us to act as creators by bringing things to the "seen or natural world" that were previously in the "unseen or Spirit world." "For by Him were ALL things created, that are in heaven and that are in Earth, visible and invisible, whether thrones, or dominions, or principalities or powers." (Colossians 1:16)

Realize we are to be one with God.

All things were created by Him and for Him. In this case *created* comes from the Greek word *barah* which means to "create from nothing." We are to create using *awsaw*, which means to "create from something." He has already created everything that will ever be needed or ever will be in our universe and is waiting for us to take our authority and manifest it into the seen world.

Realize we are to be one with God and not separate from Him. We know that everything is composed of energy and we create matter (seen) from this energy (unseen) through our belief (faith) that it can be done. God has given us the power to do this! We realize that we are connected to everything through God since God is in everything and that it is only an illusion that we are actually separate from one another. Since we all come from one source, we are all part of that source (God) and therefore part of each other. We realize that God is not *my* God or *your* God, He is just God. He is the God who will not be put in a box (calf, church building, religion). He is the God who chooses to reside in us.

You must realize that your thoughts will be transferred into things by the focusing of those thoughts, the belief in those thoughts, and the words you speak. You must realize that it works every time with *no exception*. You created it by your beliefs. If you have the faith of a mustard seed, you can command that the mountain be tossed into the sea and it will be so. (Matthew 17:20)

Reason why you are creating. What is the purpose for wanting it? The purpose should be greater than you. Ask yourself, why do I want this money, influence, house, etc.? As Psalms 35:27 says, "Let the Lord be magnified, which hath pleasure in the *prosperity* of his servant." In this case, prosperity means shalom. You should create all these things for *His glory* and

> *Don't figure out how it will happen.*

the betterment of mankind so that the world may know *Him*. You, as His child, honor Him so that the entire world may see God through you. Jesus said in John 17.1, "Father the hour is come to Glorify thy son that thy son also may Glorify thee."

You must further understand that your conscious mind, or your left brain (as many instructors call it), is your "thinker." The subconscious mind, heart, or right brain is your "creator." This is where the power lies, where the Holy Spirit dwells. The creator (right brain/heart) does not care what the thinker thinks; its only function is to make the thinker right. You must "take every thought captive" and see if it lines up with what the Word says. If it does, then plant the thought in the good soil of your heart, where it can be nurtured and grow. You must then focus these thoughts through meditation because "focused thought is the food for ideas" and it must line up with the truth because "What You Focus on You Serve."

Remember that whatever you put into your subconscious mind, right brain, or heart and hold it to be true will manifest in your life. It works this way every time! There are NO exceptions! This is why in Luke 6:45 the Word says, "A good man out of the good treasure of his heart bringeth forth that which is good, and an evil man out of the evil treasure of his heart bringeth forth that which is evil: for out of the abundance of the heart his mouth speaketh."

When your thoughts and/or words appear to be going negative and you are concerned about what you are creating, listen to

Relax physically and emotionally.

the Words in Philippians 4:8: "Finally brethren whatsoever things are true, whatsoever things are honest, whatsoever things are just, whatsoever things are pure, whatsoever things are lovely, whatsoever things are of good report, if there be any virtue and if there be any praise, Think on these things." (Fix your mind on these things.) Another excellent Scripture to memorize from Solomon is Proverbs 4:23: "Keep thy heart with all diligence (guard your heart) for out of it flows the issues (boundaries) of life."

Release. Knowing that your desire is planted in your subconscious or heart as a truth, let it go! Trust that it is done. Do not dig up your seeds of thought to constantly inspect them. Let them grow and create. When you truly know it is created you don't think on it or act apprehensive toward it any longer. You walk, talk, and act *as if it were already done*. This is faith, the faith that brings the unseen into the seen; or as the quantum physicist says, "This is collapsing or popping the quiff."

KEY: One of the toughest parts of creating, but necessary to master, is to stop trying to dictate "how" it will be done. This is key. The "how" will come about. Your focus should be seeing yourself in the done, finished, completed place. Again, you are creating an environment of peace, love, and joy around the image of you in this done place. God is a gentleman. He will not supersede your will. If you tell Him how, you limit His abilities and increase the time for your desire to manifest.

Why put limits on God when Ephesians 3:20 says, "Now unto him that is able to do exceeding, abundantly above all that we ask or think, according to the power that worketh in us (Holy Spirit)." The word *abundantly* uses three words in the Greek to describe what it truly means (*Huper, ek, perissos*) which translates to **"over and above and superior to; from out of place, time or cause to super abundance."** This is the abundance I dare to step into when glorifying my God. Don't figure out "how it will be done" just "how it looks and feels" in that place of having your desire fulfilled. Turn the "how" over to God and know what belongs to you. The only delay that can be experienced is the time that exists between you speaking and creating and the time it takes for you to truly accept your desire as truth and spiritually getting yourself ready to receive it.

Many times we desire a thing that our vessel (flesh) cannot handle. There are too many weeds to steward and rule over such a thing properly. The desire would end up running us over. Does this

> *Release knowing that your desire is planted.*

mean the answer is no? Absolutely not. The word *desire* means "of the Father." If this desire lines up with the Word, then God wants it for you. Unfortunately, His answer will be yes. Why is this unfortunate? Because, in order to steward over this desire, you will go through trials to clean up the junk in your heart. You must pull up the weeds to properly house the desire. He did not say no, He said yes, and not yet. He loves us so much He doesn't give us more than we can handle and what could lead us away from Him. He gives us what drives us closer to Him. (I will discuss this further in another chapter.)

Let's recap the process of bringing the unseen to the seen:

Relax – and create an environment of love, peace, and joy

Recognize – God exists and is in everything

Realize – you are connected to everything through God

Reason – and know the purpose behind what you are creating/desiring

Release – your creation, knowing it is done

This simple process can set you on your way to creating a new life for you and your family and be a curse breaker for you and your children's children.

I have learned some things to be careful of while in this process. When a negative situation occurs, I have a tendency to buckle down or to be forceful with my will; thus assuming that my will or "thinker" has power. The will has no power. Eventually this tactic will overload the nervous system and stress will exist in the body. Stress is when you believe you cannot overcome an obstacle, that you are not enough, and that the God in you cannot guide you to overcome. Stress is a "no power" situation.

Stress is a "no Power" situation.

When you feel stress, STOP! Get refocused and create the outcome you want to see. This is not an excuse not to work but it helps to tie no emotion to the legwork that must be done to resolve a situation. Your job is to stay in peace, joy, and love and then do what you know to do and SEE the outcome DONE in peace, joy, and love.

A final reminder: Power flows to what is focused on. What is not focused on and ignored dies. All thoughts require food and the energy of your focus is the food they need to be brought from the unseen to the seen. If there is no food the thought, whether good or bad, WILL die.

In my case, I was so consumed with *my* success and building *my* kingdom, I focused all of my energy on it. I began to lose my wife and family. I was seeking my success for them—well, that was the lie I told myself. By focusing only on my business I began to lose those things that I cared about the most. I could not understand my wife's anger and my children's distance. I thought they were the selfish ones because in my world I must be right.

I finally spoke to a friend who walked me through the principles of focus I teach for business—but he related them to relationships. I began to focus on my wife and her love language. Her love language is very different from mine. Imagine that! I began to make my family and their needs a priority, my focus. Usually all they wanted was time with me. Almost miraculously, our marriage began to heal and we began to live in the kingdom marriage I had always desired. By focusing on the relationship, I was changing and creating a Kingdom relationship.

Whenever you desire growth and power in your business, marriage, children, and relationships you must focus on those areas. Do not think negatively. Focus on Philippians 4:8: "Finally, brethren, whatsoever things are true, whatsoever things are honest, whatsoever things arc just, whatsoever things are pure, whatsoever things are lovely, whatsoever things are of good report; if there be any virtue, and if there be any praise, think on these things."

Reason why you are creating.

Thoughts that do not receive attention will dry up and not grow in your heart. Move into your God-given power and create your day and the life God has destined you to live.

10.

PURPOSE

Why was I created?

Merriam Webster's Dictionary defines purpose as the object or reason something exists or was created or an end to be obtained. Which leads to the question: Why was I created?

For all their knowledge and wisdom, parents, friends, pastors, elders, and evangelists cannot answer this question properly—and should not. There is only One who can know the purpose of an object and that is the Creator of that thing. You must ask God your Lord and King why you were created and for what purpose. He will reveal your purpose once you seek Him diligently and seek Him first. In Him lie the answers. In relationship with God, you will know why.

In Matthew 6:33, Jesus told us a key to purpose: "But seek ye first the Kingdom of God and His righteousness and all these things shall be added unto you."

Let's translate this Scripture from the Greek:

English	Greek	Greek Translation
Seek	zeteo	desire
First	proton	most importantly and firstly.
things	tauta	all the things of the world mentioned in the first paragraph, like food and clothes

When translated from its original Greek, Matthew 6:33 reads: *"But desire first and most importantly the Kingdom of God and relationship with Him and all the things you used to fret over and seek in the world will be added/given to you, including Purpose."*

Before we can learn our purpose, we must first come to know and believe "who" we really are. In the beginning, God created (*baraw*, to create from nothing) the heavens and the earth. How did He do this? He thought of creation, planted the thought in His heart, saw it done, and He spoke: "Let there be ..." (The same way we create.)

When God wanted grass and plants, He spoke to the earth. When He wanted planets and stars, He spoke to the heavens. When God wanted creatures to live in the sea, He spoke to the water; when God wanted animals, He spoke to the earth. All creation came from the source of that creation. For example, plants and trees from the soil of the earth, animals from the earth, fish from the dirt and water of the sea. He made them (*awsaw*, to make from something that already exists). Likewise, when God created man, He spoke "to Himself". We came out of God; God is our source. He said let us make (*awsaw*) man in our own likeness and image, after our likeness and let them have dominion over the fish of the sea, and over the fowl of the air, and over the cattle, and over all the earth, and every creepy thing that creepeth upon the earth. (Genesis 1:26) So God created (*baraw*) man in His image, in the image of God created Him; male and female, he created them. We were both created from him and out of him as a spirit being (*baraw*) and made from the dust of the earth (*awsaw*).

What does this mean? Let's clarify the above statements. That we were created spiritually (*baraw*) and physically (*awsaw*) in God's likeness and image. Within and without we were created both spiritually and physically in His likeness and image. We have all power, dominion, and authority over all things on earth because God Himself created and made us and we came out of God and are a piece of Him that represents Him on this planet.

We bring order to chaos.

Can we handle that? Can we believe it? I know man fell, but he was redeemed by Jesus and put back in the position he was created for—we are created for. We bring light and life into every situation. We bring order to chaos and, with the world market in the state it is, order and light are what is needed today.

Still not convinced of your greatness, your worthiness? Daniel 10:13 shows how angels move to do our bidding in the unseen. They are our "hands and feet" in the spiritual realm as we are God's on this earth. These angels move when we command them with the "word." Not beg or ask nicely, but command them. Too many times in the Word, humans fall to their faces when they see an angel; yet the angels are there to work for and assist humans. That is why angels immediately say to people they visit to "get up, stop this worship of me for I am not worthy of worship . . . I serve as you serve." We don't worship angels! They serve us in the spiritual realm when we speak in Power. They work for us when we speak the word with authority because we are the King's children. Angels are our hands and feet in the spiritual realm as we are God's in the physical realm and the angels obey the word of God when spoken by someone who knows who he is as a Son of God.

God created the universe for our enjoyment and our dominion so we could be like Him. We are the righteousness of Christ, the head not the tail. We are an example of goodness, strength, and morality. Our light does shine brightly and we are Kings and Priests on this planet when we are in purpose.

God, by His own hands planted a beautiful garden for us to tend and created it as a spot of fellowship for His greatest creation and Himself. (Genesis 2:8)

There is more proof. Let's speak about Jesus in the New Testament. In John 17:19, Jesus says, ". . . and for their sakes I sanctify (make holy and purify) myself that they also might be sanctified through the truth." The word *sanctified* in Greek is *hagiazo*, which means purified and made holy not because of what we have done or not done but because of what Jesus has done and His great purpose. We are purified and worthy.

In John 17:22, Jesus says, ". . . and the glory thou gavest me I have given them that they may be one even as we are one." Jesus is saying that we have glory which means dignity and honor and our greatest glory is when we come together "as one" even as God the Father, Son, and Holy Spirit are one.

Finally in John 17:21, Jesus says, ". . . that thou may become one, as thou Father art in me and I in thee that they also may be one in us that the world may believe that thou has sent me."

God has created everything for a Godly purpose. He creates "no junk." Everything He creates has a reason, a why, and this purpose lines up with the bigger purpose of bringing the Body of Christ back together and being the light to the world so all can know God through His son, Jesus Christ. You are never too old to find your purpose. Our God is the redeemer of time and is not time-bound like our physical bodies. He only needs you to step into purpose and all that He has for that purpose will be yours.

There are no cop-outs, no victims, no junk, and no excuses. All are called to a purpose and that purpose is bigger than any one person can accomplish by him or herself and it will be unveiled only through relationship with God. There is no retirement or free pass in the Kingdom of God. All must participate in order to grow the light in this world. We only have 120 years to do what He has called us to do on this planet for Man and we will be judged for all eternity based on what we have done with those talents He has given us for our Kingdom purpose. Let us not "bury" those talents.

All right, we now know who we are, let's discuss why we are. We were all created for one major purpose: to have an intimate relationship with our Creator which can only be achieved through Jesus Christ. Not through Buddha, Ramah, Scientology, or religion but through Jesus and His passion and His purpose. We were created in the garden originally to have relationship with God and to work in the cool of the garden. But then, with that relationship established, an individual purpose is unveiled. That thing that you were called to do to help all mankind. That reason why all your talents and gifts were given to you.

With that said, we still must work in the garden; our garden is this planet Earth which Jesus has redeemed. In this world there is work to do. Our mission is completing what God wishes in our purpose: "God wishes that none should perish and fall short of His glory." Each of us has been forged into a unique tool for the purpose of working this garden called earth in our own unique way.

God creates "no junk!"

God has a perfect plan and our individual purpose is a key cog that complements the ultimate goal of seeing that no one should perish out of God's glory. He does not want to lose one child, not one sheep, to Satan's fate. Each of us is vital in this larger "purpose" with "our individual purpose."

How do you discover your individual purpose? In your **uniqueness**, you have talents and attributes that are not like anyone else's. Some people have the ability to sing, dance, write, or communicate with people. Some people are intuitive about others' feelings. Others are skilled at baking or building. The list of talents goes on and on. You were created with the talents, abilities, and attributes needed to fulfill God's purpose for you individually. In those talents, abilities, and attributes are your *ministry* and your reason for being.

You can find your purpose by observing your talents and being aware of the passion you feel when utilizing them. When you feel the most passionate about something, that is an indicator of a task you were meant to do, it is that thing you wish someone would fix or get right because it is so obvious to you. That thing you were created for.

Sometimes, it is the thing you have been told your whole life "you couldn't do" or "it doesn't make sense" or "it won't make you money." In reality, it is the only thing you were called to do. What naysayers are truly saying is *they* can't see how it will make money, or succeed if they tried to accomplish it—but for you it is what you were called to do, you are anointed for it and in that calling, that purpose you utilize all your talents and gifts and find that place of peace, joy and love and all abundance (Shalome) that only exists in the place and purpose God called you to. This is your Passion!

All are called to a purpose.

As Jesus had His passion, you have yours, and you can choose to either step into it or run from it. Only in that thing you were created to do will you find contentment. In this place of purpose "everything your hands touch will prosper." In this place of purpose "you rest in joy, peace, and love." In this place of purpose you "will have great abundance" that God has already laid up for you. In this place of purpose God redeems time. In this place of purpose you do not toil; you know exactly why, the true why, you do what you do and you do it from a place of love. This is the place where you are glorified so that you can glorify who you represent, God the Father.

In John 17:1, Jesus said, "Father the hour is come, glorify thy son, that thy son also may glorify thee." Jesus was stepping in and completing His purpose and in that purpose He would be glorified only so He could give all glory and honor to His Father. And that is why we *must* be glorified in our purpose. We must take on an "it's not about me" attitude in all we do. We cannot promote some false humility that stifles the growth of the Kingdom and shows our God as a God of lack but a God of overflowing abundance in our call, our reason for being in our purpose. Why are you not wealthy and abundant? Most likely you are not doing what God called you to do; instead you are doing what others or the world told you that you "should" do.

Your purpose has talents required for it and these talents come easily to you; so easily, in fact, you downplay them and assume almost everyone can do it and you typically give it away for free. You give away what God has called you to do for free, rendering it a thing of no value. NO! STOP! Embrace this talent and uniqueness and start a business with it. Learn stewardship over it. If Jesus came back today and He asked for the talent that He gave you and planted in you would He call you an evil and wicked servant because you "buried it" or gave it away for free because it had no value? I would hope we could give Him the fruits of the talents He has given us, since we have multiplied them many times over, and we could hear Him say, "Well done my good and faithful *servant*."

You might think you are on purpose because you are doing good things in your life. But, are you doing what God has called you to do? You can do things on purpose and they get done. But if you do them "in purpose," your mindset is totally different. The same task is accomplished but now it is accomplished in excellence for God's glory. Proverbs 16:3 says, "Commit thy works unto the Lord and your thoughts shall be established." Which means commit everything you do, every action to the Lord, and your intentions and plans shall be erected.

Colossians 3:23 says, "and what so ever you do, do it heartily as to the Lord and not unto men." This passage tells us that anything we do, we need to do it with our hearts and souls engaged and in the manner as it was to the Lord and absolutely not unto man-faced beings (*anthropos*). We are a God pleaser, not a people pleaser. All things done should be done as unto the Lord, not done okay or pretty good so that God will cover it by *grace*, but done in **excellence**. The Lord wants you in purpose doing His will in all things.

You cannot force a purpose into your life. Force requires an expenditure of energy. When you force, you will get tired, frustrated, and angry and further separate yourself from God, your source. Purpose is only found in power and power simply *is*. The power of your choice to step into this intimate relationship with your Creator will create joy and peace in your life and cause you to vibrate at the highest level of attracting more joy and peace into your life.

During your meditations with God, your purpose will be revealed as focus is kept on Him, and never looking at circumstances. You are now in purpose on purpose. (At the end of the book, I provide fifteen questions to help guide you to your purpose.) Remember, only in relationship with God can purpose be revealed.

Before we can know our purpose we must come to know and believe who we really are!

11.

FINDING YOUR PURPOSE

Purpose is the key to a fulfilling life.

The Body of Christ is now asking: Who am I? Where did I come from? Why am I here? What was I born to do? Where do I fit in? Why am I different? What is my potential? Where am I going? Why was I put on this planet?

Purpose is the key to a fulfilling life; without purpose life has no meaning. We might ask, "Is that all there is?"

This series of questions is designed to help guide you toward your purpose on this planet. It is by no means inclusive. The only way to truly know your purpose is to ask the One who created you. Relationship with God the Father will reveal all things. These questions are guides to focus your quest for your purpose by discovering what talents and passions God has given you. Take time to do this exercise fully and completely.

Questions:

1. List five things you love to do; list them in your order of preference.

2. If you had the education, and money was not an object, what would you do as a career?

3. What are you passionate about doing?

4. What are your hobbies?

5. What sort of volunteer work do you perform?

6. What skills and talents come easily to you?

7. What is it that comes immediately to your mind when you ask yourself "Why am I here?" Write down the first things that come to your mind. Quickly! Don't think—write!

8. What do you currently do to make a living?

9. What do you love about the job you currently have?

10. What is it that makes you feel total peace or very much at ease when you do it? Be specific.

11. When you first get up in the morning there are days when you are excited and other days when you are not. Think deeply about what made you excited about the upcoming day. What made you feel apprehension or fear towards the day? Use as much space as you need to answer these two questions.

12. Describe your best friend in detail (at least 30 words).

13. Describe your worst enemy in detail (at least 30 words).

14. Describe who you are in detail (in at least 50 words).

15. What job or business would you be doing right now if you could get up tomorrow and start it, at whatever salary you feel you require? Be specific.

16. Who or what circumstance(s) is stopping you from doing the career that you want to do? Explain in detail.

After you have thoroughly and honestly answered these questions, you will be closer to discovering your purpose. You will see patterns and with the guidance of the Holy Spirit you will see which answers give you the most excitement and energy around the doing of "that" thing.

For further aid in purpose discovery, go to my website: www. nickcastellano.com and email me your questions. Remember your daily relationship formula and ask God for your specific task. First, get into a state of peace, joy, and love (see page __). When you are there, go to God's throne and ask for the vision of your future; start to see it in great detail. When you have completed this vision, write down the details. (Habakkuk 2:2)

No, it doesn't make common sense but men using common sense got us to where we are today. Our goal should be Godly wisdom not common sense in the Kingdom.

Share your discovery with a friend, a family member that will edify not crush, or your mastermind group—someone whose heart wants to see you do well and step into purpose. Do not cast your pearl among swine (those that do not want to see you succeed) for their duty is to belittle what you do because they do not want to grow or look at themselves and what "they should" be doing for the Kingdom.

Focus on the vision you have written down first thing in the morning and at night right before you go to sleep. Commune with God and your purpose and your next step toward that purpose will be revealed to you. God will give you the desire of your heart. *Desire* here means "of the Father." He put that desire there so that you would feel incomplete and unsatisfied until you stepped into it.

Then, get ready for the ride of your life—if you have the perseverance to grow as the vessel to properly steward over this purpose. Never quit because quitting is all about you and your comfort. This is all about serving the purposes of the Kingdom of God and doing what you were created to do. In that purpose is your kingship, your priesthood, all the promises of God and your shalom rest. Dare to seek it through relationship with God and once you've seen it, dare to persevere until it manifests and you have become the right vessel. Through trials and situations you will learn to steward over your purpose with a royal wisdom and a not-about-me attitude.

Please, as a part of the Body of Christ, I ask that you not cheat us out of what God wants to give all of us through you.

12.

TRIALS

It is not about you.

You have learned how to find and pursue your purpose in this garden we call earth. You now know that you have all power, dominion, and authority in this purpose on this earth and that your purpose is unique and you were created like you are to do what you were called to do. You are a King and a Priest in that purpose. You have fellowshipped and become intimate with God and in that intimacy He has revealed to you your "why." You have seen yourself in that place of doing what you were called to do through vision, and as Habakkuk 2:2 says, you have written down your vision and explained it in great detail. You have learned how to create things and conditions in your day and now that you have purpose and are on purpose you are a threat, a danger, to the Kingdom of darkness. That's right. Now that you have become this powerful being with purpose and you know who you are and where you are going and God has said yes to this desire of your heart, you enter the wonderful time in your growth process known as *trials*.

"Trials!?" you say. "I don't want trials! Why trials?"

Trials are a necessary part of your walk in purpose because trials are what eliminate the weeds from the garden of your heart. Joshua made a treaty/pact with the Gibeonites while he was deceived. (Joshua 9:15) In doing so, he allowed a tribe of "ites" to dwell in the land God had given him and these "ites" prevented the ultimate prosperity God had in mind for Israel.

We cannot make a treaty with the "ites" in our hearts. They must be ripped out, driven out, so that we can become vessels to hold the purpose and vision God has given us. If we force this purpose upon ourselves and are impatient with the process, we will be like a bowl with cracks and holes. When the metaphorical hot soup is put in the bowl it will leak everywhere and burn the owner of the bowl and drive him or her away from God, not closer to God.

An example of this would be someone who won the lottery but has not made his vessel, his heart, able to steward over this wealth properly. He has not pulled out the weeds of lack and the weeds of unworthiness and the holes of emptiness have not been filled, etc. (Statistics show such a person will hold onto his or her newfound wealth for less than three years.) The so-called winner typically ends up in worse shape financially than he was before he won the lottery. He may now be divorced, financially broke, and miserable all because he had flaws in his vessel and wealth was "thrust upon him" when he was not able to steward properly over that wealth.

God's will is that you do all things with Him. That you co-create with Him. That you pursue the purpose He has given you and created you for and pursue the road "with Him!" Anything that drives you away from Him, He does not want for you. If you are seeking God because you are "in pain" then the moment you are out of "pain" you stop seeking Him. You are now in comfort; you have some money, some power, and some health . . . why do I need God now? Note: God does not tempt or test you as the Bible states in James. You just become available for the tester (Satan) to access based on the "ites" you allow to dwell in your heart.

Once you reach the point that you seek Him diligently in all you do, no matter how much He has given you, you are then ready to step into fully what He called you to do. He knows, like David, that wealth, health, power, and money do not mean that much to you; they are just the fruits of the purpose God has for you and these fruits do not distract you from your longing for God, His presence, His fellowship, His guidance, and His love. Wealth with no trouble added to it is the fruit of your love relationship with your Papa God!

Let's now discuss the book of trials, James, in detail to see what the Word says. James 1:2 it says, "Count it all joy when ye fall into divers temptations." Initially, this made no sense to me. Why would I be happy about this? Once again, I decided to translate this Scripture from the Greek:

English	Greek	Greek Translation
count	hegomai	to command
joy	chara	calm delight
ye fall into	peripipro	surrounded by
diverse	poikilos	various manifold
temptations	peirasmos	putting to proof

When translated from its original Greek, James 1:2 reads: *"Command it all to be calm delight when you are put to the proof and surrounded by various and manifold circumstances."*

James is telling us that we have the power to keep ourselves in joy (our choice) no matter how dire the circumstances may look around us. You must not be swayed by what you see but command joy in your life no matter what. I liked this translation so much more than what the English words said to me, which was basically "Be happy as you get punched in the head." The Greek translation was empowering.

I proceeded to translate every verse in James from Greek so I could know the true meaning and purpose of the trials I was going through. I will not bore you with a word-for-word translation but I will translate the message in James. If you would like to look up the translations for yourself, and I advise you to do so, then you can see the truth in what I write and what was revealed to me:

James 1:3 says, "knowing that the trying of your faith worketh patience." It translates to: "being absolutely resolved that the testing of your trustworthiness and conviction and reliance upon Christ fully accomplishes (fashions like a tool) cheerful endurance." Wow! This makes sense: that we are to learn cheerful endurance and reliance upon Christ and what Papa God has already done for us in purpose through this test.

> *Now that you have purpose and are on purpose you are a threat to the Kingdom of darkness.*

James 1:4 says, "but let patience have her perfect work that ye may be perfect and entire wanting nothing." This translates to: "moreover let cheerful endurance hold complete mental and moral growth through this toil, that you may stand complete mentally and morally and whole in every part absent of nothing, not even one thing." That is why we have trials, so we can be complete mentally and morally and be able to properly steward over the immenseness of our God-given purpose.

James 1:5 says, "if any of you lack wisdom let him ask of God, that giveth to all liberally, and upbraideth not, and it shall be given to him." When translated, this passage reads: "moreover if any person is absent of spiritual or worldly wisdom let him beg, crave, call for this from God that brings forth to all bountifully and without defamation and chiding (scolding) and it shall be committed to him." The word *ask* in Greek is *aiteo*, which means to beg, crave, desire, call for, require. We don't just say, "God, please grant me wisdom in this circumstance" and then go on and say, "Well, God's not talking to me. I guess I'll just do ____" and fill in the blank with your worldly answer. No! We must beg and crave from our very essence. Know He has the answer and His answer is the perfect answer. He has laid it up for you for a time such as this. Stop blaming God! Read the Word, learn the Word, and you will know how to find the power in the Word.

James 1:6 says, "but let him ask in faith nothing wavering, for he that wavereth is like a wave on the sea driven with the wind and tossed." Yes, this means what we think it does. It translates into: "also let him beg, crave, desire, call out in reliance upon Christ and in consistency never withdrawing from or doubting this because he that withdraws and doubts resembles a surging and raging wave of the sea tossed with the wind and agitated."

James 1:7 says, "For let not that man think that he shall receive any thing of the Lord." Translated it reads: "but let not that type of *man-faced being* imagine that he shall take hold of any thing whatsoever from the supreme authority."

James 1:8 states, "A double minded man is unstable in all his ways." This translates to: "a two-spirited man or two-faced being vacillating in both *opinion and purpose* is inconsistent in every journey he takes." In other words, how you do one thing is how you do every thing.

I believe James 1:6-8 are the most difficult passages for us. We hear the world tell us one thing and the Body of Christ tells us another; we begin to question our purpose. We do not think we are worthy and we spiral down to a place of "no power." This is a place of being a victim, not the place of a king or a priest. James 1:6-8 says we must constantly respect our positive affirmations of "who we are in Christ" and consistently read the vision of our purpose (Habakkuk 2:2) and "why we are." These are our anchors to prevent us from being tossed to and fro. We should stay focused on the prize, not the circumstances. Day and night and/or whenever you doubt, read these passages until you again remember who and why you are.

"It is not about you!" It is about what you were created to do in the Kingdom of God. You are not a wimp, you are a warrior, which is why you have armor (see chapter 13). If you don't have a positive affirmation paper and you don't have your purpose (your why) written out as discussed in Chapter 11, then stop crying, go do what you were told to do, and write them out. If you don't, then you *have* made a choice! You have chosen to stay in the wilderness, to be less than, to play the role of victim and not victor. You always have a choice . . . make it now!

Okay, I am slowly climbing off of my soapbox—but I hope you feel my passion on this. WE are not to just continually read books to gain knowledge, we are to be wise and do these things that we know to do *in faith*. This is what pleases God. Faith is an action step. You must *do* to have Faith!

> **We can not make a treaty with the "ites" in our heart.**

Moving on to James 1:9-11, these verses talk about how everyone, from the humble (low degree) to the rich man (abounding in wealth), go through trials. James 1:12 states, "blessed is the man that endureth temptation, for when he is tired, he shall receive the crown of life which the Lord has promised to those that love Him." Translated, it means: "supremely blessed and well off is the individual (note that "man" now means a true man not a "man-faced being" after the trial) that perseveres through adversity and testing for when he is approved and found acceptable he shall take hold of and be amazed by the laurel wreath of royalty and life of which the Lord has promised to those who love Him unconditionally (*agape*)."

Once we make it through the test by relying on God and His promise to us, we move into our royalty, our kingship. After we have persevered, God knows He can trust us to steward over the purpose He has designed for us and that we seek God even when everything and all circumstances are positive and abundant. We become unconditional seekers of God's wisdom in all circumstances.

Initially Solomon was this kind of man. He sought God's wisdom to help him govern God's people, and Solomon became the wealthiest man ever to live on this planet; that wealth was a fruit of walking in his purpose with Godly wisdom.

Who brings trials to us? James 1:13 explains, "let no man say when he is tempted, I am tempted of God: for God cannot be tempted with evil, neither He tempteth any man." Translated this passage means: "let no man say when he is scrutinized and put to the test that I am tested by God because God is not temptable with wickedness nor will He tempt any man."

James 1:14 states, "but every man is tempted when he is drawn away of his own lust, and enticed." Translated this passage means: "moreover every man is scrutinized and disciplined when he is enticed and dragged forth because of his own love of self and longing for what is forbidden and then entrapped by it."

James 1:15 says, "then when lust hath conceived, it bringeth forth sin, and sin when it is finished, bringeth forth death." The translation is: "afterward, when longing for what is forbidden is arrested, captured, and planted, it produces offense, and offense to the Lord when it is consummated generates and brings forth death."

We bring these trials onto ourselves due to the lusts (weeds) in our heart. And it is okay. It is what is supposed to happen. During trials we can see the weed and choose to remove it and have life or we can choose to tolerate the weed or make a treaty with it, like Joshua did with the Gibeonites, and have death. It is our choice.

Proverbs 25:28 says, "like a city whose walls are broken down." Translated this means: "He that hath *no rule over his own spirit* is like a city that is broken down and without walls."

This process is like building a kingdom. It is supposed to happen because you have been given a word, your purpose. Mark says, "Persecution comes for the sake of the word."

Satan wants to steal your purpose and your vision. That is his job. Satan is the tester, the tempter. He was the covering cherub of God but he was fired from that job and now he is the tester. He is not after you, he is after your *purpose*. His job is to keep you from stepping into that purpose because when you do, it shortens his time on this earth and gets him closer to the pit and the fire of everlasting torment.

We all go through trials. In 1 Peter 4:12 it says, "beloved think it not strange concerning the fiery trial which is to try you, as though some strange thing happened to you." Peter is telling us trials happen and we are simply supposed to stay the course.

For a man with purpose, trials are the next step to achieving the crown of life and kingship in his purpose. When you are going through a trial, when all "hell" is breaking loose around you, what do you do? Where do you go for help?

13.

ARMOR OF GOD

Once you step into purpose, you are at war.

In Ephesians 6:10, Paul prepares us on what we need to do when we go through the trials of James. He shows us how we will don the "armor of God" purposely each and every morning. We are to start our days as a kingdom warrior.

Once you step into your purpose and start walking your God-given path, you are at war. Satan knows he has lost your soul but he does not want another warrior "on purpose" fighting against him and his kingdom. Satan wants to keep Christians as babies and victims who ask God to do it.

How can God do what He has given you power to do through relationship with Him? It is your job, not God's. He has already done it all and we are His hands and feet to accomplish it here on earth. By walking in your purpose you have decided to become a mature Christian and take responsibility for yourself and for the building of the Kingdom of God. You will not become diverted from your path of purpose to fight erroneous battles. And if someone or something dares to stand in your path to maturity, you will be capable of defeating it with the tools and armor God has given you in Ephesians.

Let's take a closer look at what Paul says in Ephesians 6:10: "furthermore my brethren be strong in the Lord, and in the power of his might." From Greek, this translates: "furthermore my brothers be empowered and enabled in your relationship of rest with the Lord, and with your relationship with the Holy Spirit who is God's power wielded by you in forcefulness." Paul is telling us that we should be at rest. We should keep our attitude of peace, joy, and love; that in this rest and our intimate relationship with God the Father, we can wield the power of the Holy Spirit, and this Holy Spirit power is God's might (or force) on this earth demonstrated through us.

> **Put on the whole armor of God that ye may stand against the whiles of the devil.**

In Ephesians 6:11, Paul writes: "put on the whole armor of God that ye may be able to stand against the wiles of the devil." When I translated this from Greek, I discover: "slip into the full armor of God as it becomes a part of you not separate from you so that it might be possible to continue to establish God's purpose toward and forward moving over the trickery of Satan." When we don the armor in peace, joy, and love it becomes part of us and leaves nothing exposed. We and the armor are one and with this armor we can continue to move God's purpose forward and plow over the trickery of the devil.

Ephesians 6:12 says, "for we wrestle not against flesh and blood, but against principalities, against powers, against the rulers of darkness of this world, against spiritual wickedness in high places." When translated from Greek, the message is clearer: Because we wrestle (vibrate is the actual word) not moving forward toward people, but we vibrate positively forward and toward magistrates, move forward and toward super human control, forward and toward Satan, forward and toward demonic plots and schemes in celestial or heavenly places. You see we are on the offense and when we wrestle we actually "vibrate" in a positive vibration with a high frequency and this vibration is generated toward the unseen places and principalities controlled by Satan not toward people. As we vibrate or wrestle, we are constantly moving forward and toward the issues and problems because we know that "the gates of hell shall not prevail against it (the church)." (Mathew 16:18.) You see, gates are defensive in nature and we are to be on the attack against the kingdom of Satan; not hiding behind the walls of our church praying for the rapture. Our attitude should be one of occupation not evacuation.

Ephesians 6:13 states, "Wherefore take unto you the whole armor of God that ye may be able to withstand in the evil day, and having done all, to stand." The translation from Greek is: "Focus and channel the act of receiving the full armor of God so that it is possible for you to stand against and oppose in the vicious, malicious, hurtful day, and having donned the armor to oppose this day completely be stanch and establish your God-given purpose." Wow! Did you get that? Read it again until you understand it: "establish your purpose" is what the actual translation means. There will be a hurtful and malicious day but because we have donned our "full armor" we have the ability to establish our "purpose" on this planet. To establish a purpose you must know what that purpose is or you will be tossed like the wind and the waves.

Paul goes on to tell us what the full armor of God is, what we should look like in this armor, and what the function each piece of armor has. Ephesians 6:14 states, "Stand therefore, having your loins girt about with truth, and having on the breastplate of righteousness." Translated, this means: "Completely by standing and establishing your God-given purpose, having your procreative power fastened around you on a belt, and this belt is truth (what the Word says; not what the circumstances around you say), and the protection plate for the chest of our justification."

Know that Jesus redeems you to make you righteous and whole in the eyes of God. In Ephesians 6:14, you protect your procreative power by only hearing and speaking the truth (the Word). You are not double-minded and you do not listen to other people or the whispers of Satan. You listen to the Word and speak only in truth. Also, you protect your heart with the breastplate of righteousness knowing that your heart, through Jesus and His death and resurrection, has given you permission to go to speak with God **directly** and know intimately His heart and that in this relationship of righteousness you will not lose on your journey in purpose knowing that God always completes what He has started.

Ephesians 6:15 goes on to say, "And your feet shod with the preparation of the gospel of peace." When translated this means: "and your feet tied up and bound under the feet with the preparation of the good news of peace and prosperity." Everywhere you walk, you now bring an environment of peace and prosperity with you. You become an environment changer for the Lord and you are a king and a priest in that environment.

_____

... speak to God directly and know intimately his heart.

_____

Ephesians 6:16 states, "Above all, taking the shield of faith, wherewith ye shall be able to quench all the fiery darts of the wicked." This means that, most importantly, the armor is a shield (a large, door-shaped shield) of reliance; that God can and will do what He says He will regardless of circumstance. With this shield you shall be in power to extinguish all of the ignited and glowing missiles of those people who mean evil or hurt to you. With the shield of faith you are blind to the circumstance because of its dimensions and every evil circumstance fired at you will be put out because you know what your God has said will happen, must happen. You only need to stay the course and remain focused on Him and His purpose for your life.

Ephesians 6:17-18 states, "And take the helmet of salvation, and the sword of the Spirit, which is the word of God: Praying always with all prayer and supplication in the Spirit, and watching there unto with all perseverance and supplication for all saints." This translates into: "cumulatively accept the encirclement of the head (helmet) for defense and the dirk (a knife about eighteen inches in length used for hand-to-hand fighting) of the Holy Spirit, which is the Rhema word of God. Supplicating and worshiping at every possible occasion, with all worship out loud and petitioning in the Holy Spirit and staying alert to the Holy Spirit with total persistency and prayer for the other fellow saints."

This section amazed me when I realized the sword of the Spirit was not a long sword used in King Arthur's day but rather a knife used for in-fighting to get underneath the armor of the enemy. This tool is for when the enemy comes "face to face" to test your conviction to what God has promised you and this offensive weapon can "lash out" and cut your enemy so that he must retreat.

In these passages it states that the sword of the Spirit is the "Word of God." Basically, you reply with the Word whenever adverse circumstances or lies present themselves to you, just like Jesus did when he was tested in the desert by the devil. Based on your faith in the power of the Word, you determine how effective this offensive weapon will be against the enemy. Are you a circumstance believer or a God and His promises believer?

When I am face to face and in a battle, my belief in the Word may be a bit weaker than I had hoped. I may have glimpsed at a circumstance or two. So, I turn over my body (flesh) to my spirit and allow it to pray the *perfect prayer* in the tongues of the Holy Spirit. This prayer is not weakened by my mind or what I think or feel. It bypasses all of that because I have surrendered to the Holy Spirit. It is the perfect prayer for the situation and gives my dirk great power to attack and wound the enemy.

If you don't believe in the use of tongues or think tongues were only used in the apostles' days, then stand on the Word of God with all faith. Don't let the utilization of tongues take you out. I would encourage you to do more reading in the Word so you can see that the utterances of tongues is for the here and now, the perfect prayer for today as you go through the fire.

In Ephesians 6:19-20, Paul continues: "And for me, that utterance may be given unto me, that I may open my mouth boldly, to make known the mystery of the gospel, For which I am an ambassador in bonds: that therein I may speak boldly, as I ought to speak." Oh no! Not more of that word *utterances*. Let's go back to Acts 2 and investigate a little.

Acts 2:3 states, "And there appeared unto them cloven tongues like as of fire, and it sat upon each of them." Acts 2:4 states, "and they were filled with the Holy Ghost, and began to speak with other tongues, as the Spirit gave them the utterance." This is when tongues entered the New Testament. On Pentecost the apostles were filled with the Holy Spirit and received the ability to wield the power of God which was made evident by their speaking in tongues.

> ... *the sword of the Spirit is The Word of God.*

If God is the same yesterday, today, and forever, and He used tongues to indicate the power of the Holy Spirit in man in AD 1, then why would tongues not also be available to those who have the Holy Spirit dwelling in them today? (If the concept of tongues makes you angry, get over it. Keep reading; don't speak in tongues but believe what you do speak comes from a place of faith and not of fear or an I'm-pretty-sure attitude. Read 1 Corinthians 14:2-4.)

When translated Ephesians 6:19-20 means: "And for me, that the right words in Faith may be given to me by the Holy Spirit, so that I may open my mouth (*stoma*, front or edge of a weapon) in boldness, frankness, and assurance to certify and declare the secret of the Good News, over which I am an ambassador or representative positioned in chains of choice; and in this position of representative I will be confident and bold in what I say and do this speaking in the manner necessary for speaking in power."

Words have power. God created this universe by the Word and everything that we see in this world is held together by His Word. We were created in God's likeness and image and as Christians the Holy Spirit dwells in us and our words have power.

When you speak you create. Quite simply, if you speak on positive productive things you create positive things in your life and the lives of others. This concept is not a joke, not a game; this is how it works in the unseen. You think, you believe in your heart, you speak, you create the reality you and yours live in. If you don't believe this, you lose by default, you become a victim, and you become part of someone else's creation, someone who understands the power he wields with his words.

Life and death are in the power of the tongue; as Deuteronomy 30:19 states, "I call heaven and earth to record this day against you, that I have set before you life (strength, freshness, merriness) and death (pestilence and ruin), blessing (prosperity) and cursing (vilification): therefore 'choose life,' that both thou and the seed (fruit, seedtime, children) may live."

The choice is yours, choose now or by making no choice you have chosen "death." (Note: there are more than 110 Scriptures in the Bible that refer to the tongue, its power, and the power of words. There might be something to this . . .)

14.

VISION: A KEY TO CREATING

What you focus on, you get more of.

What is vision? When I was five years old and living in Alexandria, Virginia, a girl my age and I were playing barbershop in the basement of the apartment complex where we lived. She was cutting the front of my hair when the scissors slipped and ruptured my eye. All the contents of my right eye spilled out. My parents rushed me to the emergency room where I was immediately admitted. A doctor looked at the eye and said it could not be saved. He recommended a glass eye be installed. My father got angry; he would not receive this report. He said to the doctor, "No I don't accept this." My father asked the doctor what he would do if it were his son.

The doctor was compassionate and said he would put a patch on my eye and give me eye drops to use to keep the eye from becoming infected and see if the eye would heal. My dad agreed to this treatment.

We were to follow up with the doctor in two weeks to see how my eye was doing. My mother diligently put the drops in my eye three times a day and she would constantly have to keep my hands from the bandage. Every day my parents prayed to God to heal my eye and they had friends and family pray as well. In two weeks we went back to the doctor's office. He removed the bandage and the eye was whole and healed. My vision was tested and found to be 20:40 with no depth perception problem. It was a miracle for a boy who almost lost an eye. My parents would not accept the bad doctor's report and because of that I have two healthy eyes today.

> *"We must have vision so we do not perish."*

The vision I could have lost would have been the natural vision of one eye. However, there is a much greater concern in the Body of Christ . . . it is the possibility of losing our "creative vision."

What is creative vision? That is vision with the power to create your future. It is the vision that builds individuals, builds wealth, builds cities, and builds nations. In Proverbs 29:18 it says, "My people perish due to lack of vision."

We are becoming blind in our creative realm. We cannot see with our mind's eye where we are going. We can only see what we have, where we have been, and where we are now. "What you focus on you get more of." If we keep focusing on what we already have, we will continue to get what we already have.

We are like a young boy with scissors in both eyes, blind to the power our creative vision holds. Our potential energy (stored energy) is enormous but it cannot be released to kinetic energy (energy in motion) until we have a vision of where we are going, what we are creating, and how beautiful that place will look. We need to become blind to the adverse circumstance of what we see (which is what we already created unknowingly), and focus on purpose on what we want to create and draw into our lives.

The How-To of Vision

The Business World—When thinking of starting a new venture, the first thing you would put together is a plan that describes how you see the business. This plan forces you to look into the future of the company and what you should see over the next one year, five years, and ten years. A key part of the business plan is the pro forma which creates a format that looks into the finances of the business and allows adjustments to be made before the business starts so they are not catastrophic for the business in later years. A one-year plan and a five-year plan are crucial for business development.

The Secret–*The Secret* is a bestselling book and DVD which tells you how to create your reality. It gives little reference to God or credit to Him that He is the One that created the process. *The Secret* over-simplifies the process, however the concepts taught in it are a critical part of creating in your purpose. Part of the key to the vision process in *The Secret* is feeling how it feels when you are in that "positive result" and sending out those positive, attractive, energy waves so that what you think about and feel about will be drawn to you (Law of Attraction).

There are two significant tools utilized in this process. The first is a "vision board." Post pictures of what you desire on a corkboard and put it in a place where you can see it every day. We think and create in pictures. If I say the word *elephant*, in your mind you don't see the letters e-l-e-p-h-a-n-t, you see a large gray animal with a trunk. By looking at the photos on your board daily, you will constantly see what you desire until you are comfortable enough to allow yourself to receive them. It will be drawn to you once your subconscious sees it as done.

The second technique is meditating on the things you desire from a feeling of gratitude. Take time each morning to focus on those things you desire. See yourself with that new car, new house, new baby and also the *feeling* of having it already. This emotion attaches energy to the desire and enhances the attractive forces to bring you what you desire in a quicker fashion. There is no work to be done. Just think it and feel it and it is so.

The Word of God–Before I discuss what the Word says about vision, let's get something in line that has been out of order in the Body of Christ for awhile: Work is *not* a part of the curse! Work was in the garden before man fell from grace (Genesis 2:15) and it will always be here on earth and will be here through Jesus' millennium reign. Man was created to work. This gives man a purpose for living.

Life insurance companies know that on average, eighteen months after a man retires from his job, he dies. This is the cold hard fact that insurance companies count on to make a profit. Work is good and Godly and a necessary part of creating wealth in the Kingdom.

In the Word of God *vision* is found many times. For example, in Philippians 3:13-14: "This one thing I do, forgetting those things which are behind and reaching forth into those things before us. I press toward the mark for the prize of the high calling of God in Christ Jesus." We don't focus our creative vision on what is or what was, we focus on "what should or will be." We "reach forth" with our "mind's eye" into those things before (in front of) us. We continue to press forward to the mark (previously concealed idea or thing) not for us but because of our purpose (assignment) for God on this earth in Christ Jesus.

Once you have that vision "don't look back!" In Luke 9:62, Jesus said, "No one who puts his hand to the plow and 'looks back' is fit for the Kingdom of God." In other words, once you have your vision stay focused on it and don't go back and forth seeing pictures that cause fear and faith. If you do, then don't expect "Kingdom of God" results. The Israelites, due to their looking back to Egypt, made a thirteen-month trip to the Promised Land last forty years. Stay focused on the results that you want, not on the circumstances that appear. When you see your vision then you must be committed, both feet in, not one foot in the world and one in the Kingdom. A double-minded man should expect nothing.

As Christians we must have vision so that we do not perish. (Proverbs 29:18) The word *vision* means revelation or Godly creative vision and the word *perish* means naked or uncovered. With that being translated, the verse now says "where there is no Godly vision my people are made naked and uncovered." We are susceptible to the plans of the world and the plans of Satan much like when Adam and Eve sinned and realized they were "naked and uncovered." They were no longer under God's spiritual covering.

George Bernard Shaw knew this concept. He said, "You see things; and you say, 'Why?' But I dream things that never were; and I say, 'Why not?'" President John F. Kennedy used this same sentiment to birth the Genesis and Apollo space programs. Robert Collier said cross the bridge in your mind *before* you come to it. You see, Christians are essentially visualizers for the Kingdom of God and this visualization makes us actualizers. If we can visualize something and not faint from it, then we *will* see it come to pass.

> *"And the Lord answered and said write the vision and make it plain upon tablets, that he may run that readeth it."*

The faith step, the action step, carries your vision over the goal line even though it is too big for you. (Or so you think.) Once you make the commitment to do what God has called you to do and you do not look back or look at circumstances, the resources and people to see your vision through will appear.

In 2006, *Fortune Magazine* polled executives of Fortune 500 companies and asked them the characteristics they look for in employees. The results are as follows:

Vision 35%

Ability to energize people 33%

Communication 19%

Charisma 8%

Competence 5%

The number one trait they look for in new employees is vision. With vision and a faith in that vision anything is possible.

Finally, one of the key verses in the Bible about vision and how to create from vision is in Habakkuk 2:2: "And the Lord answered me and said write the vision make it plain upon tablets, that he may run that readeth it."

Because this passage is often misunderstood, let's see how it reads when translated from Greek and Hebrew:

The Lord answered (said pay attention to me, Habakkuk had been complaining) and said write (engrave) this (Godly) vision, make it plain (explain it completely) upon tablets (or paper), that he may run (when someone else reads your vision and understands it because he knows it is truth) that readeth (proclaim it out loud) it.

This verse is about explaining your vision fully and in detail so when someone you trust reads it it will make perfect sense and he or she will support your vision and get on it and proclaim it out loud to others. Having key people see and agree with your vision is important; the power of agreement is tremendous.

15.

VISION AND PURPOSE

With vision your purpose brings forth fruit.

Without purpose in your life you have little spiritual vision. In Proverbs 29:18 the Word says, "Where there is no vision, my people perish." In Lamentations 2 we learn that vision is from the Lord.

There are many types of vision in purpose and there are distinctions in each type of vision. Let's discuss the four different types of spiritual vision in the Word and how they relate to purpose.

First and most important is the vision (*chazon*) of mortal sight, a dream or revelation. This is when you see with your spiritual eye what you should stay focused on when creating your day in purpose. (Daniel 8:2)

Second is the vision (*march*) of seeing something come from the Holy Spirit. (Ezekiel 11:24) You have been given a vision by the Holy Spirit for a reason or a purpose.

Third is the vision gazed at (*horama*). Visions should be spoken of often with no fear. (Acts 18:9) Do not be in awe of your vision; on the contrary, speak of it often and do not hold back.

VISION AND PURPOSE

Fourth is the vision one receives when in a trance (*machazeh*). This vision is received with your eyes open, you are awake but you see someone or something not of this world. (Numbers 24:4)

These four types of spiritual vision are keys to the identification of your purpose and the fulfillment of your purpose. What you focus on you get more of, so you must focus with your eyes on what is the truth, plant it in your heart, and speak what you see in your heart, thereby attracting and creating more of the same.

In purpose you must learn how to discipline yourself to your spiritual vision so you can get detailed and specific information; focusing on what is not and bringing it into this matrix you have created in the physical world. You must focus on it day and night and see it complete in your vision and write it down so that your eyes can see it and you will speak of it, thus bringing it from the unseen to the seen.

And, when it is written down clearly, others will read of it and when two or more people are in agreement and of one mind, synchronized in thought on a situation, it must come to pass. This falls in line with the Old Testament account of the city of Babel. The Babylonians had a single vision as a people, a single purpose to build a tower. In Genesis 11:6, God states the most amazing thing: ". . . and now nothing will be restrained from them, which they have imagined to do."

The word *nothing* in Hebrew is *kol kol* which means "all, any or every." Nothing?! Wow! When we are in agreement as one nothing is impossible.

The only problem with these people and their vision was that they did not build the tower for the glory of God. God was not part of their plan, so He "confused their language." But the principle of agreement and single-mindedness on a vision is still in effect and active today. When two or more are of one accord and come into agreement together, it will be done. You see, you simply steward over the vision you've been given, it is not for you or about you, it is for others. You were created to serve both God and others and in that service is your authority. Do not be disheartened if the vision does not manifest immediately for with a "Godly vision" that is part of God's ultimate plan and purpose. It will occur exactly at the moment it should.

Habakkuk 2:3 tells us: "for the vision is yet for an appointed time, but at the end it shall speak, and not lie. Though it tarry, wait for it; because it will surely come, it will not tarry." To understand this verse completely, the Hebrew must be utilized. The beginning portion of this verse means your vision that God has given you has an appointment, a precise moment when it is to occur. It should not be forced. Force is about you. Force takes energy. Stand in power; power just is. During this waiting time, you will be walking in the vision, seeing it done, and growing personally with Godly character, so you can be a good steward over this immense task God has called you to. The time delay is needed so the vision coming to fruition does not destroy you. You can develop into the vessel that can hold this vision and steward over it properly.

> **When we are in agreement "As One" nothing is impossible.**

The second portion of the verse, "but at the end it shall speak," means at the last apparent moment it shall break through and not fail. When it looks most bleak and very dark with no change, it will not fail. The next phrase, "though it tarry," means that although it appears to hesitate in the time table you would like it to happen in (*tarry* in this case is the Hebrew word *mahahh*). "Wait for it, for it will surely come" means exactly as it says, but the word *come* (*bo*) is used twice to emphasize the fact that it will come to pass.

The final part of this verse says "it will not tarry." (What? Just nine words earlier it said it will tarry.) The word *tarry* in the second use is a different word. It is the Hebrew word *achar* which says "it will not be late." It will happen at the exact moment it was to happen, in God's perfect timing, so He can have all the pieces moved into place. As your vision comes to pass it creates a domino effect of amazing positive events.

VISION AND PURPOSE

When you read the Word, I encourage you to translate the passages from the Greek and Hebrew so the full meaning, not what you've been told by someone else, is revealed to you. It is your responsibility, not your pastor's, priest's, deacon's, elders' or anyone else's to learn and study the Word. The Word has a unique message just for you and this message cannot be given to you if you don't pursue it yourself. (For easy access to the Greek and Hebrew translations of the Bible, you can receive a free download for your computer at www.e-sword.net. No more excuses. Learn what the Word really says so you can empower yourself to do as it directs you.)

The first time I saw the magnitude of my vision, as revealed by the Holy Spirit, it was too big for me. How could I do this thing? He must be talking to someone else! In the vision, I saw me in front of two thousand men— teachers, preachers, evangelists, pastors, and trainers. I was to teach the teachers a common language and a common pur-

It will happen at the exact moment it was to happen.

pose so that we could communicate with each other in the Body of Christ and reach the same destination to accomplish the same goals "As One." By uniting those who come in contact with tens of thousands to millions of people each year, we would be uniting the Body of Christ. We would have a common vision (the vision of heaven on earth), a common purpose (to bring Kingdom rule and reign back to the planet) through the power of love and a common language. We would not focus on our different religious beliefs but rather on our similarities in Christ Jesus and learn the language of the Kingdom of God, not a religion. Once again, we would be as the City of Babel "and now nothing will be restrained from us that we have imagined to do." The difference this time is we won't build for our glory, we build selflessly for God's glory—as it should be.

We, as the Body of Christ, are too fragmented in our goals and desires for God. We have no unity. We are split into religions and within the religions there are churches and within the churches there are groups (different ministries) and within the groups there are clicks. Each segment out for its own purposes and what suits it best and each segment with its own beliefs and language and purpose. This is especially true in some evangelical communities where the church (ecclesia) is run like a small business. The decisions that are made are made for what best suits the ecclesia's needs and not the needs of the big "C", the Church/Body of Christ. Each ecclesia has its own language and its own purpose and the larger purpose of the Body of Christ is barely considered in the decisions the local ecclesia makes. Most churches can't even meet their Biblical mandate of providing for widows, orphans, strangers, and the priests!

"What is best for me and mine" is the place where decisions are made and this attitude further separates the Body. Churches of the same denomination actually compete and fight with each other for parishioners and are afraid to send their flock to be taught a needed concept at another church for fear of losing their people. Losing their tithe! What are we doing? Who is our provider?

Pastors are to train and release the flock into the world so they can bring light and life to their world outside of the church walls. It is often forgotten that we are God's people and we are called to do His purposes.

For now, let me say I saw my task as daunting; not possible for me. But He did not plant it in me for me to do alone. He wants to do it with me just as He wants to join with you in your purpose. We must rely on Him and with that reliance He will bring the resources and the people to help us accomplish what we are to do—what we have been designed for, purposed for. All we have to do is the legwork and to persevere.

Never, ever, quit or settle for less than your whole vision! You will find as you persevere, you pull closer to God and as you pull closer to Him your character grows so you are able to steward over the mighty vision God has given you.

VISION AND PURPOSE

When you step up and begin to create the things in life you know you were called to do, your mind starts to buzz and gets in the way of your creating by bringing up the past. The apostle Paul experienced this issue and left us some valuable information on what to do when it happens. In Philippians 3:13-14, Paul says, "This one thing I do, forgetting these things which are behind and reaching forward unto those things which are before. I press toward the mark for the prize of the high calling of God in Christ Jesus." When there is a high calling there must be other places you can settle for in "good enough."

Once you start on your journey of purpose, Jesus says, "No one who puts his hand to the plow and looks back is fit for the Kingdom of God." (Luke 9:62) You see vision, is a key to your future in purpose. Vision is given of the spirit and planted in the heart. Do not look back to Egypt as the Israelites did. Stay focused on your purpose. Do not look for a place of comfort or safety. Step all the way in with both feet. Your safety and strength are in the Lord, not in some safe circumstance you may have created for yourself. Stay focused on your Promised Land journey.

As has been said by others:

- You see things; and you say, "Why?" But I dream things that never were; and I say, "Why not?"
  (George Bernard Shaw)
- Cross the bridge in your mind before you come to it.
  (Robert Collier)
- Our aspirations are our possibilities. (Robert Browning)
- Cherish your vision and your dreams as they are children of your soul, the blueprint to your ultimate achievement.
  (Napoleon Hill)
- Where there is no vision the people perish.
  (Proverbs 29:18)

With vision, your purpose brings forth fruit and you can offer that fruit to the Body of Christ. As stated before, our God is a God of purpose and everything He has created has a unique purpose, including you. Purpose is key to a shalom life. Without vision and purpose you will be frustrated and unfulfilled.

As Dr. Myles Monroe teaches, "When purpose is not known abuse will occur." *Abuse* is broken down into two words: *abnormal use*. We are abusing ourselves. We are struggling to force ourselves to fit into the world's system while still trying to maintain our relationship with God through Jesus Christ. We are not *of* this world. We are *in* this world but we operate from a higher system. We are subjects of the Kingdom of God and in that Kingdom there are laws that supersede the laws of this earth, including the way business is done. We must dare to step into this Kingdom way of doing things—the world needs us to awaken now, more than ever before.

The world's systems are falling apart and people are looking for the light. "Where is the light?" they say. "Where is the salt?" When we look just like the world, smell just like the world, do business just like the world, pursue the things the world pursues, then we are no different than the world. We give up our kingship and our priesthood and relegate ourselves to blend in with the masses, to find comfort and to be a respecter of people not God. In Galatians 4:1, Paul writes: "Now that I say, that the heir, as long as he is a child, differeth nothing from a servant, though he be lord of all." In this instance, the Greek word for *child* is *nepios* which means a non-speaking infant or a simpleminded person.

Without purpose in your life you have little spiritual vision.

We are infants knowing the truth but afraid to speak it. We are simpleminded; expecting God's blessing but living the world's way. We must take accountability for this planet and its condition—for we were given stewardship over it and yet we "hide our light under a basket" (church building) and do not profess what is correct to the world. We are at fault when the thief came while we slept and were comfortable. We are responsible for abortion laws being passed, God being taken out of schools, gay marriage being sanctioned (love the people yet hate the sin), and our God through Jesus Christ slowly being bled from our nations. We can blame only ourselves, the ones who have been given all power, dominion, and authority. We act like children, victims of some evil thing happening to us instead of us acting "as one" in love and taking back for the Lord that which he has given us to steward over. We must remember we are the light of the world not the church (little "c"). We are the "ecclesia," the "called out ones." Not the "called into the church ones" but we are called out and into the world to guide it. We, the people, are the "salt of the earth" not the salt of the church building.

It is time for us to set things right. The planet's systems are failing, as it was meant to, and we are to be the cream rising to the top, prospering when the world and its systems fall apart. And when the world asks us how we are doing this, how are we creating wealth, how are we prospering when all else is falling apart, we can *show* the world by giving all the glory and honor to God through Jesus Christ.

In John 17:1 it says, "Father the hour is come, glorify thy son so that thy son may also glorify You." The time is now! The time to seek God and step into purpose is now!

> **"Awake, o sleeper, and arise from the dead and
> Christ shall shine upon you and give you light."**

16.

SPIRIT MAN: THE HIGHER EXISTENCE

As a spirit being you are complete, lacking nothing.

Proverbs 9:10 says, "The fear of the Lord is the beginning of wisdom and the knowledge of the Holy (*gadoch,* God eminence) is understanding. Understanding is realizing that you are truly a spirit being connected to your God always and that He lives in you and that as this spirit man you are perfect once you accept Christ into your life and experience the indwelling of the Holy Spirit in you.

Wow! What does that mean?

If you, as a spirit being, are whole and complete, lack nothing and are living in an environment of love and peace, why do you spend so much time and why does the church spend so much time focusing on repairing, rooting out, and cleaning up the soul (mind, will, and emotions) when all you need to do is allow yourself to exist as "spirit man?"

Reason with me, if you will. Presently in the church and in many self-help seminars, much of the focus is on cleaning up our "stinking thinking" or rotten programming. Your mind, your thoughts, and the things that were put into you as a child formed your identity. These concepts are now affecting your adulthood and the fruit of your existence. You spend time aligning your Will with what you say you really want and try to avoid self-sabotaging your goals by aligning your mind and will. You focus on the emotions and energy you put around your thoughts so as to give these thoughts power by creating an emotion that activates your hypothalamus. This releases a neuropeptide which keylocks into every cell of your body thereby causing your body to vibrate at the frequency of that thought and emotion. This activates the Law of Attraction and brings to you what you truly desire, manifesting it in your world as a reality. If you do all these things just right and do not allow circumstances to influence you in any way or diminish your belief (faith) that this event or desire can be done and that you are worthy (no double-mindedness now) to receive it, then it will be so.

Whew, that was a mouthful! I don't know about you but to me that seems like a lot of work with too many opportunities for your mind, will, and emotions to lose their focus and allow your desire not to manifest.

In the above scenario, the mind is playing a very active role in the manifestation of your desire and attempting to keep you (as is its duty) in the past or project you into the future; never allowing you to be in the "now" where it loses control. So, this method, in my opinion, is destined to failure a majority of the time. But it will sell books, because *common sense* says it should work.

Let's talk about an easier method. As a spirit being, you are complete and lack nothing. As a spirit man you are love and this love is your power and is as God created you to be from Himself in His likeness and image. Spirit man's emotion is constantly in joy or, if you will, in a state of (*Chara*) calm delight. Our spirit man lives in a place or environment called Peace (Hebrew: *Shalom*, Greek: *Eirene*), whole and complete in prosperity, lacking nothing.

If it were possible to turn control of who you are over to your spirit man and quiet your mind then you would vibrate at an extremely high frequency. This high-frequency vibration would continually attract people, places, and things that would continue to produce joy, peace, and love into your life.

> *"The fear of the Lord is the beginning of wisdom . . . "*

The question is, how do you access this spirit man and turn control of who you are over to your true self? The key lies in the time of Now!

17.

THE NOW

The key to power, dominion, and authority.

The Now. What is "The Now?" Is it just another New Age term that has no place in the life of a Christian or is it more?

In Exodus 3:14, the Lord God spoke to Moses on the top of Mt. Sinai. When Moses asked what is the name of God, He said to Moses, "I am that I am. I am has sent me unto you." I am? What a name. I Am. Why would God call himself I Am?

God was telling Moses the state, the location, and the place where you can find God. In "I Am." God would not let Himself be identified with a name, label, or a form (as evidenced by the golden calf incident). God just is. He is always "in the is/now." He is always I Am.

Let's return to Genesis. When God created the world in which we live, he would speak to the item to bring forth life in that item. For example, when he wanted life in the sea he spoke to the sea, the source of life in the sea and that source brought forth life. (Genesis 4:20) When God brought forth life on the earth he spoke to the earth (firm land) and it brought forth every living creature on the earth after its own kind. (Genesis 1:24) However, when God made man, He made him in His own likeness and image. He spoke to Himself, "Let us make man in our image after our likeness. And let them have dominion." (Genesis 1:26)

You must learn to control your mind and thoughts.

So we were made into God's likeness and image and came out of God himself, our source who spoke to Himself to create us. We have been given dominion over this earth He created for us and we are to subdue it (Hebrew: *kabash*–to conquer, subjugate, keep under, bring into subjection).

We were created like God, by God, and have been created to have dominion over our place of residence (earth) as God does in heaven. God is the great I Am. He performs everything "in the Now." He wields his amazing power because he is always present Now. We were created in His likeness and image therefore we can only wield the power, dominion, and authority God has given us; so we can subdue this planet in the Now!

We spend too much time disempowering who God created us to be by not living and aligning with God in Now. We lose our creative ability by living our lives in regret of yesterday or in fear of tomorrow and fear that tomorrow will look just like yesterday. Remember, what we focus on we get more of so again by being in fear and/or regret while we are in the Now moment, we create more fear and regret incidents.

You must learn how to stay in your place of authority, your place of alignment with God. The only place you can do anything for anyone else is in the place of Now. To do this, you must learn to control your mind and thoughts and let your spirit man take dominion over your flesh and align you with your power. Your power is God through Jesus Christ.

When creating your day, it is vital that this exercise be performed in the Now moment or you are truly not creating.

92

18.

THE NOW KILLER

The mind creates a never-ending stream of mental "noise."

We tend to be slaves to our minds. It is the duty of the mind to keep us living in the past or project us into the future where, as beings of Now, we have no power. By doing this the mind has control over what we do, how we feel, and most importantly who we are. The mind creates a never-ending stream of mental noise that prevents us from finding the peace, love, and joy that can only be found in Now. In the Now, in the place of I Am, we wield the power, dominion, and authority bestowed on us. It is the duty of the mind to keep us living in the past or projecting into the future where we as a "Being of Now" have no power. By doing this constantly the mind has control over us, what we do, how we feel and most importantly WHO we are.

Man was created in the likeness of God from the soil. He was created to fellowship with God in the Now and to work the garden (this planet earth). Man was given a mind so he could solve problems during his work, come up with names for all the creatures on this planet, to help him exist. At first, man was a spiritual creature with a body and a mind to "create" solutions, if you will.

When the fall of man occurred, fear entered into man as he cowered and hid from God. The mind was already taking over, creating problems to solve.

- Problem: Adam and Eve noticed they were naked and needed to cover themselves. Solution: leaves.
- Problem: Adam and Eve noticed God was in the garden and they had sinned. Solution: Hide
- Problem: Adam and Eve were asked to divulge the truth to God. Solution: Take no accountability and blame someone else, i.e., "This woman that you gave me." (Adam blamed both Eve and God as the reason for his failure.)

We have become a "Mind Slave."

Because of this sin, the mind was now in charge. The mind, whose job it is to keep you in yesterday or tomorrow, whose job it is to continue to create potential problems so it can be busy. The mind's job is to keep you out of the Now where your spirit man is empowered and your mind quiet. It must stay in control.

This is how man lost dominion over his mind—and it is still so today. The only way to get that dominion back is by allowing yourself to live in the Now moment and quiet your brain. This is your power and the release of your spirit man. This is your alignment with God to wield His power. It can only be experienced Now.

In today's information-infested, Internet-laden world, thinking has become our greatest "dis-ease". Dis-ease occurs when things are out of order or alignment or balance. The mind, when utilized properly, is a highly specialized tool—however, today your mind is more apt to use you, which creates dis-ease and is out of order from the way you were created.

The tool has taken over; most of the time to such an extent as you allow yourself to be identified or labeled by your mind. You identify yourself based on your mind's perception of your past deeds and how it preserves present circumstances to project some future outcome.

In the seventeenth century, René Descartes said, "I think, therefore I am." This lie has permeated mankind for hundreds of years as a truth. God said, "I am that I am." (I exist because I exist.) That is how God identified Himself. Thinking was never part of His identification. We are created in His likeness and image and should not allow ourselves to be identified by what our mind labels us to be. We are told by our mind what to do, who we are, and what our future will be. We have become a "Mind Slave."

The first major step to "Awakening the Sleeper" is to know you are not what your mind says you are. You must realize that there is a vast range of intelligence beyond your thoughts; thought is only a small aspect of intelligence. The word *intelligence* comes from the Latin word *intellegere* which means to understand. Knowledge (facts, figures, memorization) is not understanding therefore *not* intelligence. Intelligence is knowledge, wisdom, and understanding.

In the twenty-first century we have relegated ourselves to the belief that knowledge is intellect and with that definition the mind, the storer of knowledge, is our master. Knowledge is only the intellect of the body.

Step into your greatness. Step into Now.

We have forgotten the other two vital components of intellect:

Wisdom is the ability to be skillful, artful, subtle, and cunning with the knowledge you have accumulated. *Chākām* is the Hebrew word. It is the utilization of knowledge with your heart. This is the intellect of the soul.

Understanding is the ability to become a separate being. To be able to separate mentally (*biyn* is the Hebrew word). In other words, understanding is of the spirit man. **It is the ability to take the knowledge you attained in the body, utilize the wisdom of the soul, and apply it properly as a spirit man as a higher being.** As this spirit man, you were created to be in common union (communion) with your God who created you in His likeness and image.

As Proverbs 17:27 says, "He that hath knowledge spareth his words and a man of understanding is an excellent (*yagar*, valuable) spirit." He that has understanding is valuable for the Kingdom of God for he knows who he truly is. Not what he thinks, not what he did, not what he feels, but he is whole and lacks nothing. He is the spirit man, existing in an environment of constant joy, peace, and love. He is not what he does—he is an extension of I Am.

Step into your greatness. Step into Now!

19.

ACCESSING THE NOW

Don't be a human "thinking." Be a human "being."

In order to move into the Now you must understand two things. First, you are NOT your mind. You are a spirit being with a soul and a body, created by God. Your body has a mind that is a tool to be used to solve this world's problems. You are not that mind. In your mind you most likely identify yourself based on your past or the projected future—not honoring the Now. The only place where you have access to God is in the Now—which is evidenced by His name, I Am.

Second, you, the spirit man, are not subject to time but have the ability to transcend time. You were created in God's image and before God created "in the beginning" there was no time. God lives in a place where there is no time. He is everywhere all at once and "every when" all at once. He is the Alpha and Omega, the beginning and the end. Time is the illusion.

I'm sure you have heard the saying "Time is precious, has great value, and should not be wasted." This is not quite accurate, however. What we mean to say is: "This Now moment is the only time

I have and I choose to be totally present. Now!" That sentiment is more accurate.

The string of Now moments is a precious gift from God; yet you miss the moments when you project your self into some hope of future glory or fear of future defeat. We are taught by God to embrace the journey not the destiny; to be in the Now always through up-and-down circumstances. When you are in the Now and in relationship with I Am you have nothing to fear and you know exactly who and whose you are. Remember life is Now and fellowship with God is Now. You are one with Him and all things are in communion with all things through Him Now. No other time matters but this instant and the fullness of you that you pour into this moment.

Me, the Spirit man, dictates the emotions I choose to feel and release.

To find this Now place of peace, joy, and love you must meditate daily, be quiet, and silence your brain's desire to flash to your past or project the future. In chapter 1 I discussed how I meditate every morning using breathing techniques, listening, and going to the throne room to sit on Papa God's lap to create my day. Use this technique for your benefit.

When you feel fear or stress or a heavy burden know that you have left Now and are somewhere else. These triggers tell you that you are missing it and it is time to get back to Now. Whenever I feel a burden that takes me from peace, I will pull my car over to the side of the road and stop driving or sit down in a chair if I am working, and close the door, get quiet, and breathe in through my nose and our through my mouth until I re-establish my relationship with my God in the Now moment and a feeling of peace envelops me. Once I have re-established myself in the Now with my Father, my source, I can continue with my day in peace, love, and joy.

When I first started to use this meditative technique, I would have to perform it six to eight times each day because my mind wanted to always be in control. Eventually I took charge of me. Me, the spirit man, dictates the emotions I feel and the meaning (label) I attach to circumstances. I no longer give that power away to anyone—not even my own mind.

Be the victorious spirit man you were created to be; not a victim to your thoughts. Don't be a human "thinking." You work much better as a human "being."

You are NOT your mind.

20.

A CALL TO ACTION

The Sons of God are those who walk in power, dominion, and authority.

Romans 8: 19 **For the earnest expectation of the creature waits for the manifestation of the sons of God. 20 For the creature itself was made subject to vanity, not willingly, but by reason of Him who hath subjected the same in hope. 21 Because the creature itself also shall be delivered from the bondage of corruption into the glorious liberty of the children of God. 22 For we know that the whole creation groaneth and travaileth in pain together until Now.**

In those four verses the word creature *is translated* to *Ktisis* (Greek) which means *creation*. You see, all creation is subject to man's condition and awaits (groans for) the manifestation of the sons of God to put things back in order so that the earth will look like heaven once again.

A CALL TO ACTION

The sons of God are those who walk in the power, dominion, and authority we (humans) were given. They are those who know "who" and "why" they are and have died to their flesh and have made their sole purpose to fellowship with God and to serve mankind. The day of restoration is coming and it is coming soon. All of the earthquakes, tornadoes, tsunamis, hurricanes, etc., are a reflection of man's condition on this earth. As the Word clearly states, creation is unwillingly subject to the condition of man.

Mankind is currently disjointed and at odds—like never before. There is little unity in our world. Disunity is seen in nations, politics, religion and churches, and the family unit. Nations are divided, as evidenced in the U.S. during the last few elections. There appears to be a 50/50 split between our political parties, with no common ground to unite them or the country. In the early days of the United States, the Word was used as a tool to establish common ground between political parties. That is no longer the case; it is just one view in opposition to the other. The Bible has essentially been removed from the way our country is run and we are segregated in our religions and beliefs. I am not just talking about the differences between a Muslim and a Christian either. Christians have segregated into separate sects (Catholics, Protestant, Methodist, and Baptist). And within each religion there exists separation. There is no unity in the Body of Christ, so why should the world listen to a faction that looks as disjointed and separate as the rest of the world? Even with the common language of the Word, the world sees fighting and separation amongst Christian religions, not unity. If the commonality of the Word doesn't work for "The Church" then why do we need it for a country? Get rid of it, is their opinion.

In today's evangelical church, the spirit of God is moving and causing believers to re-examine how they "do" church. The measure of a church's success is no longer about its size, spiritual gifts, or small groups but about making a significant and sustainable difference in our cities and communities, and in the lives of the people.

If we are the light of the world and the salt of the earth then we cannot keep that light under the basket of the church building. It must go out into the community and light the way and be the preservative of the cities and nations by making a difference.

As Eric Swanson says, "It is time to stop building walls and our own separate Kingdoms and start building bridges into our community." Community: *common unity*.

The church needs to fill needs in its community, regardless of the religion or belief of the people. When we see a need, we must offer our assistance and satisfy the need. This is how we take back a city for the Kingdom of God using the same tools Jesus did: love and service.

. . . within each religion there exists separation.

It is time for the local church to stop measuring attendance and begin measuring the impact it is having on its city. The greatest testimony for the reality of Jesus Christ is witnessed by what we do not by what we say. The word *preach* means to teach and to show. Jesus taught by softening the hearts of the people and then showed by healing the sick, feeding the hungry, and comforting the lost.

It is time for the church to stop talking and start preaching. It is time to start equipping the saints for the work of service in the community. We, as the Body of Christ, are the *ecclesia*, the called out ones. As the called out ones, we impact our communities through our field of choice (job, career, service). My mountain, if you will, is business. I am called to do business in the world. To preach the gospel by what I do not by what I say.

Typically there is little support or help from the local church for the businessperson. For years businesspeople have been looked on by the church as a source of income and little else. The local church will utilize a businessman who is a CPA with a doctorate in accounting as a greeter at the door. What a great use of one of God's resources: to use an individual who knows how to create wealth and manage money, in a church that needs both skills, as a greeter or an usher.

In the past, church leaders have felt it is their job to keep the flock humbled. No wonder most of the churches today are broke! They teach the concept of serve us, the local church, not service to the Kingdom and the community in which they live.

It is time to view local churches as a franchise of the Body of Christ. If the Church is franchised as the Body of Christ and each local church is a franchisee, then we should communicate with each other. Instead of each church acting autonomously, with its own budget, sales and marketing programs, and community service programs, why not come together as One and pool the resources of the local churches? Why not form a board of pastors that meets regularly to focus on making an impact on the community at large? Key projects can be identified that will impact the community and the churches can work together to make a difference. Then we begin to look and act like the Body of Christ with a common vision, a common language, and a common focus. Pastors must see their congregation as *the city* not just the small flock that meets within their walls.

Unite "As One" to manifest the sons of God.

The Church must unite, with the pastors in the lead, for the common love of our cities, our communities, and our people. It is time to unite As One and help evoke the manifestation of the sons of God. It is time to quit building our kingdoms and instead work on building the Kingdom of God, for this is what we were called to do.

Pastors, you have a platform to change our communities, cities, and nation. Help take back what is the Lord's through love and service. Do your part to make the earth look like heaven again.

Awaken O Sleeper, it is time to take back what is the Lord's and put it back under His covering.

And that time, as always, is **NOW!**

REFERENCES

Nick Castellano spent five years researching information for *Awaken the Sleeper*. The following is a list of the sources he used in his journey; he hopes they are inspiring and helpful to you.

Note: A free and easy-to-use download of Greek and Hebrew translations of the Bible, is available at www.e-sword.net. No more excuses. Learn what the Word says so you can empower yourself to do as it directs.

Anthony, Dr. Robert. 2004. *Beyond Positive Thinking: A No-Nonsense Formula for Getting the Results You Want.* Morgan James.

Arbinger Institute, The. 2000, 2002. *Leadership and Self Deception: Getting out of the Box.* San Francisco, California: Berrett-Koehler Publishers.

Arterbum, Stephen, Stoeker, Fred. 2000. *Every Man's Battle: Every Man's Guide to Winning the War on Sexual Temptation.* Colorado Springs, Colorado: WaterBrook Press.

Bristow, Mark. 2004. *Why Bad Things Happen to Good People: The Christian Promised Land.* Xulon Press.

Byrne, Rhonda. 2006. *The Secret.* New York, New York: Atria Books/Beyond Worlds Publishing.

Chown, Marcus. 2006. *The Quantum Zoo: A Tourist's Guide to the Neverending Universe.* Washington DC: Joseph Henry Press.

REFERENCES

Eldredge, John. 2000, 2007. *Desire: The Journey We Must Take to Find the Life God Offers*. Nashville, Tennessee: Thomas Nelson.

Enlow, Johnny. 2008. *The Seven Mountain Prophecy: Unveiling the Coming Elijah Revolution*. Lake Mary, Florida: Creation House.

Greene, Brian. 2003. *The Elegant Universe: Superstrings, hidden dimensions, and the quest for the ultimate theory*. New York, New York: W.W. Norton & Co.

Hankin, Mark. 2002. *11:23: The Language of Faith*. Alexandria, Louisiana: MHM Publishing.

Hawkins, David R., MD, PhD. 1995, 1998, 2002. *Power versus Force: The Hidden Determinants of Human Behavior*. Hay House Inc.

Hawkings, Stephen. Penrose, Roger. 1996. *The Nature of Space and Time*. Princeton, New Jersey: Princeton University Press.

Hill, Napolean. 1937, 1960, 1988. *Think and Grow Rich*. New York, New York: Random House.

Klemmer, Brian. 2008. *The Compassionate Samurai: Being Extraordinary in and Ordinary World*. Hay House.

Lawden, Derek F. 1967, 1995. *The Mathematical Principals of Quantum Mechanics*. Mineola, New York: Dover Publications.

LeTourneau, Del. 2007. *The Money Manual*. Mesa, Arizona: WholePoint Publishing.

Lewis, Aaron D. 2004. *Healing for the 21st Century*. New Kensington, Pennsylvania: Whitaker House.

Lin, Derek. 2007. *The Toa of Daily Life: The Mysteries of the Orient Revealed/ The Joy of Inner Harmony Found/The Path to Enlightenment Illuminated*. Penguin Group.

Mattera, Joseph. 2003. *Ruling at the Gates: Preparing the Church to Transform Cities*. Lake Mary, Florida: Creation House Press.

McCall, Richard D. 1997. *The Way of the Warrior Trader: The financial Risk-Taker's Guide to Samurai courage, Confidence and Discipline*. McGraw Hill.

REFERENCES

McElfresh, JR. 2002. *Spirit Quest: Our War with Choices.* Xulon Press.

McIntosh, Ron. 2007. *The Greatest Secret: God's Law of Attraction for Lasting Happiness, Fulfillment, Health and Abundance in Life.* Lakeland, Florida: White Stone Books.

McManus, Erwin Raphael. 2001. *An Unstoppable Force: Daring to Become the Church God had in Mind.* Orange, California: Yates & Yates.

Medearis, Carl. 2008. *Muslins, Christians, and Jesus: Gaining Understanding and Building Relationships.* Bloomington, Minnesota: Bethany House.

Meyer, Rick. 2005. *E-Sword (King James Version).* www.esword. net.

Monroe, Dr. Miles. 2004. *Rediscovering the Kingdom: Ancient Hope for our 21st Century World.* Shippensburg, Pennsylvania: Destiny Image Publishers.

Nash, Jon Oral. 2004. *First Steps of the Profitable Steward: 7 Steps You Must Take Now to Create Abundance.* Pittsford, New York: Jon Oral Nash Ministries.

Pierce, Penney. 2009. *Frequency: The Power of Personal Vibration.* New York, New York: Atria Books/Beyond Words.

Polich, Judith Bluestone. 2001. *Return of the Children of Light: Incan and Mayan Prophecies for a New World.* Rochester, Vermont: Bear & Company.

Porter, Dr. Tecoy. 2007. *Releasing Your Inner Treasure: 8 Kingdom Keys to Unlocking the Wealth Within You.* Manchester, Connecticut: Foghorn Publishers.

Pringle, Phil. 2005. *You The Leader.* New Kinsington, Pennsylvania: Whitaker House.

Riddle, James. 2006. *The Complete Personalized Promise Bible: On Financial Freedom.* Tulsa, Oklahoma: Harrison House.

Smith, Windell. 2006. *Marketplace Ministeries: Pastors and Business Leaders in Kingdom Partnership.* Seattle, Washington: The City Church of Seattle.

Smolin, Lee. 1997. *The Life of the Cosmos.* New York, New York: Oxford University Press.

REFERENCES

Strong, James. 1890, 1986, 1980. *Strong's Concordance.* Chattanooga, Tennessee: AMG Publishers.

Wilkinson, Bruce. 2003. *The Dream Giver.* Sisters, Oregon: Multnomah Publishers.

Winston, Dr. Bill. 2006. *The Kingdom of God in You: Discover the Greatness of God's Power Within.* Tulsa, Oklahoma: Harrison House.

Zacharias, Ravi. 2000. *Jesus Among other Gods: The Absolute Claims of the Christian Message.* Nashville, Tennessee: W Publishing Group.

CDs

Aragon, Art. Dr. 2008 series. *How to Last in the Last Days*

Hagee, John. 2004 series. *Blessed and Highly Favored*

Harrison, Bob. 2007 series. *Power Points For Success.*

Millman, Dan. 1997. *Way of the Peaceful Warrior*

Munroe, Myles. Dr. 2008. *The Power of Purpose*

Nash, Jon Oral. 2008 series. *Prosperity Scriptures*

Renner, Rick. 2008. *Sparkling Gems from the Greek*

Thompson, Jeffrey. 2005. *Brain Wave Suite*

What The Bleep (Down the Rabbit Hole). 2007.

Winston, Bill. 2005 series. *The Blessing of Abraham*

Winston, Bill. 2008 series. *Heaven on Earth*

Winston, Bill. 2006 series. *Reality of Redemption*

ABOUT THE AUTHOR

Dr. Nick Castellano is passionate about each individual finding their "why" and their God-given purpose in life. He is recognized as an implementer of ideas and strategies and has been instrumental in the startup of more than 400 businesses. He is the director of Business Mentorship International (BMI), a mentoring program that offers how-to's for owners of businesses at all stages of development.

With a master's degree in biochemistry and ten years as an instructor of nuclear power chemistry for the U.S. Navy, Nick knows he has a unique ability to break down complex issues into understandable language for all to comprehend. Nick went on to receive his doctorate in Psychology and Religion.

He is presently the holder and creator of two oil well enhancement patents and principal in three oil and energy companies that do business throughout the world. For this reason he is a highly sought after speaker, mentor, and consultant for businesses, corporations, conferences, and churches.

He resides in the Phoenix area with his wife, Michele, and their two sons. Together they empower people everywhere "on purpose."